MINISTRY
Traditions•Tensions•Transitions

William J. Bausch

Foreword by Anthony Padovano

TWENTY-THIRD PUBLICATIONS

Mystic, Connecticut

First printing   April 1982
Second printing   April 1983
Third printing   August 1984

Edited by Marie McIntyre
Book design by John G. van Bemmel
Cover design by William Baker

Library of Congress Catalog Card No.: 81-86345

For Florence,
who touched Life

Mark 5:25-34

On the wane
Woman with a hemorrhage, fading by the hour.
Once, serpents bore you through the sea
bejeweled with foam,
charged and bright with laughter.
But now, you are beached,
serpents dead at your feet.
You chart your diminishment daily.
Unclean, lost,
beyond the purview of God!
Friends drop off their pets who have died.
And there is Jesus,
hub of the widening crowd.
"He's like the serpents and the sea," she thinks,
"He is my true self—
Oh life, if I could touch you again!"

(her poem)

Foreword

It is a privilege to introduce this splendid book. *Traditions, Tensions, Transitions in Ministry* is written in a clean, concentrated style that belies at times the depths of meaning it reaches. It is a book which synthesizes at least a half century of significant research on the biblical and historical roots of ministry. It expresses a lifetime of wisdom from a man whose personal sensitivity and pastoral experience give him every right to address this topic. The book is gracefully written, a pleasure to read, challenging in its content, and creative in its proposals for parish and ecclesial reform. It is a remarkable blend of the practical and the profound.

There is a correlation between pastoral ministry and theological awareness. Theological awareness enables a minister to realize options that are at times crucial to the work of ministry. The less one knows, the more likely it is that he or she will offer the same advice and the same solutions for everyone. Ignorance has a way of limiting life.

The minister represents the church on an intense level of its life. This requires that the minister devise strategies which he or she believes are correct and which also fall within the range of Catholic life. People seek out a minister not only for human contact and wisdom but also to know how their lives can be nourished by Catholic experience. A minister who knows little or no theology will prove unimaginative and unhelpful. A lack of theology may leave the minister to his or her native liberal and conservative instincts. A minister with severly limited theological knowledge deprives people of the care they deserve.

It is obvious that William Bausch has studied, read, and reflected through a lifetime of pastoral responsibility. He sees, therefore, different ways in which the church may proceed and still remain a church faithful to Christ and to its apostolic foundations. He knows too much to suggest that the church must forever repeat its past in much the same form that the past was lived. He is aware that ministry has even a much wider context to work in than its present expansion allows. The church of the early centuries provides a model for ministerial reforms and opportunities that it would be a tragedy to ignore. Father Bausch is able to summon and certify people for so many diverse ministerial functions because he knows his history so well, his church so thoroughly, the imperatives of the present so vividly. Historical awareness prevents us from wasting the present.

This is an important book. First, it is important for Father Bausch to have written it. The writing must have demanded a good deal of reading and reflection. William Bausch has read widely and caught the unstated implications of the history and books he has made his own. His writing must confirm for him his sense of the different directions he can move his parish without failing to give it the life it expects from him.

It is rewarding to see a pastor who can do full-time ministry and find the opportunity for such impressive research. Actually, ministry and research support each other. The time needed to write this book is a gift of ministry to the people of his parish. His book challenges all in pastoral ministry to deeper theological awareness for the sake of a more pastoral life. The book makes it clear that pastors can bring an impressive dimension to theological writing. Theology is not meant to be an academic discipline perfected in direct proportion to one's distance from people. Theology, preaching, ministry, and prayer are creatively related and constantly reinforce one another when they are properly experienced.

Secondly, this book is important for the people who will read it. It offers ecclesial ministers an unparalleled opportunity to conduct their ministry imaginatively. All the biblical, pastoral, and historical data one might need to live out a ministerial vocation responsive to church in the fullest sense of the word are present. Father Bausch manages to give us the past and the present. He is critical but never caustic, intelligent but fully concerned with the pastoral options that intelligence brings. He is unafraid of history and contemporary problems.

I recommend the book enthusiastically. I encourage the reader to make notes, underline significant sections; and return to the book many times. I suggest that the reader owes gratitude, as I do, to a priest whose ministry enriches our own.

Anthony T. Padovano, S.T.D., Ph.D.
January 15, 1982

Contents

Introduction

The word *ministry* has not been immune to the denaturing process that overuse and misuse always promote. It seems it can be "in" or "out," "hot" or "cold," according to the phases of the moon. The danger here is that such a good biblical word, with roots in the New Testament, might fall into blandness or disuse. It is too strong a word and concept to allow that to happen. It is too meaningful for the church of today to let it float along on the popular culture stream, because it is precisely around this concept that much of the current change in the universal and local churches will occur for a long time to come.

This book, then, is written to keep the word *ministry* in focus. It is written for the average educated Catholic who will not read heavy treatises or indepth theological books but who still wants some background, some sense of direction. This is for the person who wants to know how the history and theology of New Testament ministry translate into the every day, parish situation of his or her own life.

To try to meet these needs, this book is divided into three parts. Part I, "Traditions," covers in four chapters the history and theology of ministry from the first to the fourth centuries. These chapters show us the progression of our traditional triad of bishop, priest, and deacon as well as the regression of popular lay ministries of considerable variety. Part II, "Tensions," takes all of this past history and theology and, in three chapters, introduces them to the present. Then it stands back and examines the very real tensions arising from the collision. It examines the serious theoretical conflicts between institutional and local church as well as the practical nitty gritty conflicts between clergy and laity as they meet for the first time in mutual uneasiness. Part III, "Transitions," takes two chapters to examine the local parish, and how real applications of a collaborative and shared ministry can be made there. Finally, there is an appendix which includes some very practical examples listing a large variety of sample ministries and ministers and a census form that both discovers needs and invites participation.

This book is intended to be a companion volume to *The Christian Parish: Whispers of the Risen Christ* (Mystic, Ct.: Twenty-Third Publications, 1980). It is not necessary, of course, to read that book together with this one, but it would help a great deal and provide a wider vision. Meanwhile—and it's a long and gracious meanwhile—thanks are due to the people of my parish community who minister to me daily, to those who listened patiently to the ideas in this book and who made them real and to Carol Rodeck who typed the manuscript with patience and diligence.

CHAPTER ONE

A Variety Of Ministries

—1—

As they were being driven from the Garden of Eden, Adam remarked to Eve, "My dear, we are entering into a period of transition." This splendid understatement could be taken as the motto of the Catholic Church these days—these years—after Vatican II. While we must honestly say that there are signs of great vitality, freedom, a remarkable persistence of prayer and faith, an upsurge of interest in scripture, and a new sensitivity to social issues, there are also crises and plenty of them. There is a noticeable distancing from the church's official teaching, a serious erosion of discipline among both active laity and clergy, complaints about poor liturgies and worse preaching, the alienation of youth, family breakdown, and a severe decline in numbers of priests, religious, and seminarians. These are only some of the issues that preoccupy the church and sap its energies. There are more.

The underlying principles of Vatican II have not been seriously applied and its challenges perplex us today. The way-we-look-at-church has not always been seen in its light. Common Christian symbols are being undermined by sophisticated commercialized symbols of the mass media and consumerism. We don't seem to have a common popular theology that binds us together.

11

We're more apt to talk in secular pop psychological terms when discussing the great questions of life. Our gurus are not the saints or the theologians, much less the popes. They are the talk show personalities and scientific "experts." For many there is no clear understanding of what it means to be a Catholic, no firm distinctions from anyone else whose religion is just as good as ours. There is confusion between hierarchy and democracy as synods, national conferences and parish councils struggle to draw the lines of authority (and power?). And there are the explosive issues ranging from divorce and abortion to married clergy and women's rights in the church.

Simply to catalog such things is to know in one's heart that it's all true, that we are indeed in some kind of terrible transition. Perhaps one of the more visible signs of so much of our questions, conflicts and perplexities is the whole question of ministry. This is because this issue more nearly touches all of our Catholic lives. Yet, like so many other issues, the whole question really seemed so simple at one time. What was the problem?

Ministry belonged to the hierarchy who in turn got it by ordination. The priest was one who, though inferior to the bishop, shared in his powers to some degree. Deacons were not around. At the courtesy of the bishop, laypeople might do some things considered apostolic. In the 40's, 50's and into the 60's this was called "Catholic Action" and was officially described as "the participation of the laity in the apostolate of the hierarchy"—Pope Pius XII's phrase. There was therefore no ambiguity. Ministry belonged to hierarchy, hierarchy lent some of it out on occasion. Now it's all up for grabs.

Clarity is gone. There is talk today that all Christians are called to ministry and all equally, so that one does not in fact derive his or her ministry from another or participate in anyone's apostolate; rather, one derives ministry from baptism. Laypeople are now filling roles formerly considered the preserve of the clergy. Clergy are having an identity crisis as evidenced in the 30,000 who were laicized during the pontificate of Paul VI and the drastic decline in the numbers of young men seeking the priesthood. If, in our confusion, we run back to the sources for clear directions to interpret all of this, a respected and eminent theologian reminds us quite bluntly, "Revelation does not give us a clearly articulated notion of ministerial priesthood, the bible does not offer a clearly defined view of the essence and forms of the Christian priesthood, and does not furnish a detailed and fixed concept of the ministry.''[1]

A key sign that any culture or society is really in the midst of profound change is the inability to define things. Ministry, which was hardly ever used popularly until a few years ago, is just such a word. Today it means so much and so little. Because it is fluid, it indicates a cultural and theological shift. Ministry therefore becomes less a concept than a symbol of an ideology—and one not shared by the official Catholic religious establishment, lay or clerical.[2] Let us look at this more closely.

There was a time when everyone knew what we meant when we said the word *priesthood*. Today, it can also mean the priesthood of all believers. Once, only the priest possessed the official ministry of the church. Today, everyone possesses it through baptism. Once, ordination was the privileged power which conferred the fullness of the active ministry. Today, baptism takes priority and ordination is seen as an aspect of that. Once, the essence of the Catholic priesthood was seen in the personal power a male received at ordination to consecrate the eucharist and forgive sins even apart from community. Today, this is seen as departure from the first thousand years of the church's understanding which held that presiding at the eucharist is the result, not the cause, of presiding over the community. Once, office was an automatic status conferred from above by ordination and the office bearer, by that very fact, was leader, with authority and power. Today, the functional ability and charism of any baptized person take emotional precedence over the status of the professional clergyman as ministerial competence replaces mere status. Once, power and authority were pyramidal, moving downwards from the pope to bishops to religious to laity. Today, power and authority are respected only when seen as yielding to personal giftedness and collegiality. In short, if yesterday's world was a world wherein priesthood was well defined and pivotal and ministry of the people was vague and residual, today's world is just the opposite.

Now, most or all of these concepts and ideas are not necessarily true. We put them forth here for two reasons. One is to show how much different thinking is going on in the area of ministry (lay and clerical) and, secondly, to underscore that many of the notions presented here form the investigation of this book. Something is happening, for instance, when the number of seminarians decreases and the number of men and women interested in church ministry, but not the priesthood increases. Something is happening as diocese after diocese establishes commissions on lay ministry or nonordained ministry and colleges and universities offer more and more courses in lay ministry. Something is happening as some seminaries train not only candidates to the priesthood but also lay people, both male and female, in the same classrooms at the same time.

It is this "something" that the following pages seek to explore. Here is an attempt to investigate the question of ministry by starting at the beginning, by moving through history and theology and ending at the current questions and adjustment crises we are going through right now. Understandably there are many questions. Understandably there are no easy answers. Still, it is always of great benefit to have a sense and a context of the questions. Right answers, after all, can only come from right questions. So let us begin.

—2—

To find out what the origins of Christian ministry are, we must turn to our normative founding documents, the New Testament. Not that this means we are bound to draw exact parallels between what we find there and what we should therefore imitate in our own times. That would be stagnation. On the contrary, we are basically trying to discover there principles which both guide us in right directions, give us mandate for development and yet keep us faithful to the original apostolic witness. As we look, however, we must remember that we must jettison any preconceived notions about church structure and ministry we may have.

We moderns are so confidently aware that power filters down from universal papacy to local clergy with jurisdiction parcelled out along the way. We are vaguely conscious of the historical threefold division of bishop, priest and deacon. We are officially assured that this is the way that Jesus left this precise pattern to his church. But do we find this in scripture?

No, not quite. When we turn to the New Testament pages, we discover that Jesus did not directly institute bishops or priests or deacons in either the ancient or modern senses of these terms. In fact, we should rather be struck with the irony that the only real form of structure we do find Jesus himself directly connected with promptly disappeared shortly after he did! Most scholars agree that Jesus himself picked out twelve laymen as his twelve apostles, a reflection of the fullness of salvation for all humankind, a kind of twelve tribes of Israel of the New Age. When Judas died, the eleven filled up the gap by the election of Matthias, but there it ended. When Peter died or James, John or Andrew or any of the others, there was no attempt on the part of the early church to replace them or to keep the twelve going as a distinct numerical institution. In fact, with uncommon suddenness, the twelve are not mentioned again after the death of Stephen. They quickly disappear.

It would seem that persecution broke up the twelve and the Jewish Christians had to flee from Jerusalem. We might surmise that since the whole concept of the twelve is so basically Jewish, modeled after the twelve tribes of Israel, there was no inclination to keep such a foreign notion going when the church moved to the gentile world. Therefore, the early Christians turned to other forms to hand on the apostolic tradition. This is a clear indication that Jesus obviously did not provide a blueprint for his church. He left his intentions, genius and desires but gave the church total freedom to develop what forms would best fulfill these hopes.

There is that section in the gospel (Lk 10:1-12) where Jesus gives very exact instructions to the seventy-two disciples to go and evangelize. It's a carefully laid out program. Yet here too, even though originated by Jesus, there is no attempt to replace the seventy-two as an institution. Finally, there is that other ministry we are sure of from scripture: the origin of the seven so-called deacons (Acts 6:1-3.) But it is clear that these seven developed into much more than waiters on table. In reality they became a new band of travelling apostles and took over many of the original functions of the twelve apostles such as leading prayer and preaching.

We all remember "deacon" Philip and the Ethiopian he evangelized and baptised. We remember "deacon" Stephen who preached and was killed for his witnessing efforts (if not for his long and boring speech). So we see that the various ministerial responsibilities of the twelve apostles, the seventy-two disciples, and the seven deacons—all found in scripture—were quickly distributed among others such as, as we shall see, the prophets and the teachers. For example, Barnabas and others are described in the New Testament as "conducting the worship of the Lord and fasting" and teaching and proclaiming the inspired word of the Lord in the liturgical assemblies.

The point that comes across is that from the beginning of the new church the controlling ideal of ministry seems to be the communities' needs arising from their grounding in Christ and the apostolic tradition. *Any* structure that serves this ideal is legitimate. The church did not consider itself bound even to forms that Jesus used. Rather it took from him that perfect freedom to build up his body, the church, and to proclaim the Good News in those forms and structures that best seem to do the job. This being so, we should not be surprised to discover in the New Testament and contemporary Christian writings a great deal of fluidity in ministry and leadership and no absolutely fixed forms of either. That would come later after the church settled down; until then the catchword is development. That is why, back in 1971 when the United States bishops were looking into all of this, they asked a group of New Testament experts to look through the sacred scriptures and give them the results of their findings on this whole question of ministry and the primitive church. Here is part of that report.

> From what has been said it should be evident that we can expect to find in the scriptures an evolution in the concept of ministry that is eminently in keeping with the nature of a pilgrim people of God.... It will mean, first of all, that we cannot use the Old Testament as a primary referent for our conception of christian ministry .... Acceptance of the concept of evolution will mean, secondly, that even in the New Testament we should not expect to find a clearly formulated definition of christian ministry from the beginning, or at any simple single point in the development of New Testament revelation. Christian ministry was never "frozen" in any one mold but continued to develop and to be adapted in the succeeding moments in history. This does not mean that there is no normative character to the New Testament canon. But the normative character will not be seen in definitive "canonizing" of one exercise of ministry without regard

for another, or of one historical manifestation at one time or place in isolation from other such manifestations. Development itself is canonical and therefore normative.[3]

This bears careful reading, especially that last sentence. The statement speaks of evolution and development and so alerts us to the fact that we are not going to find any clear-cut patterns in scripture or in the early centuries of the church's existence. Again we are also alerted to be cautious about canonizing any one form as eternal and unchanging. The church came up with many ministries, some permanent, some temporary, all adaptable. This is perhaps best demonstrated by Saint Paul's image of the one body with many members. This means that primitive ministry is being shaped by the needs of that body and not the other way around.

—3—

Before we proceed further, we ought to pause for a little and necessary reflection. We have mentioned the New Testament in the preceding pages. It might be well to recall that it is a compilation of some 27 short booklets written over a period of some 50 years and not started until about 25 years after the death of Jesus. Written by anonymous authors, except for some epistles attributed to Paul, the New Testament writings reflect various geographies, theologies and mentalities. Knowing this prepares us for the diversity in ministry we shall meet.

There are also, however, some contemporary *non*-New Testament writings that are helpful—though far too few and some in fragments at that. They carry, for the most part, authentic names that sound strange to our ears for such names reflect ancient Greek and Roman times. It is good for us to be acquainted with such names and we will make several references to them. There are the *Letters of Clement of Rome,* the work called the *Didache* or sometimes the *Teaching of the Twelve.* Both *Clement* and the *Didache* were written at the end of the first century and therefore at the same time as some of the later New Testament writings. There is the book called the *Shepherd of Hermas,* the letters of Ignatius of Antioch (Syria) (d. 117) and Polycarp (also from Asia) and the works of Ireneaus of Lyons (d. c. 202), Cyprian of Carthage, Justin, Clement of Alexandria, and others—all authors reflecting the second and third generations of Christian practice and belief.

From some of the city names attached to these authors we see that Christianity spread quickly around the Mediterranean Sea. Reflecting on this can perhaps help us adjust our mental images of how our religion was started. For many Catholics, the image of Christianity is that of a seed planted in the ground. Jesus placed the seed there and then the trunk grew and then the branches grew up toward the sky in one straight line. If we want to trace our religious heritage, all we have to do is start at the top of the tree and work downwards until we come to the apostles, (the roots) and then Jesus (the seed). It's a simple cause and effect chain and all doctrine and styles and structure can be traced to the unity of that simple backward process. This analogy is faulty because it gives the impression that there was strict unity from the beginning—one large seed planted and one large tree its result. But the facts are otherwise.

Indeed, a better image might be that of a stone tossed into the middle of a pond. It has simultaneous ripple effects all along the shoreline and furthermore, the ripple of water configures itself to the shape of the shoreline it touches. One place is even, another full of curves, another among reeds, another shallow, another deep. Christianity is like that. Jesus is the stone or, as some call it, the Christ Event (Jesus as a complex of revelation of the Father, his whole redemptive work, his message, his teaching, all that he is). Jesus was tossed like a stone, so to speak, into the Mediterranean Sea. The Christ Event washed up all along the shores, and different peoples and shorelines received, responded, and configured differently, preserving different traditions about Jesus. In short, there was a variety of traditions about the impact of this Christ Event from the beginning. We can see this so clearly in the four gospels, which preserve the same traditions in different versions or different traditions altogether. Different emphases appeared from the beginning; even different theologies. And, as might be expected, different structures of ruling, leadership, and ministries. This accounts for the diversity we shall meet in our exploration.

So, keeping these reflections in mind, we take a second look at the early traditions that give us the expected picture of much variety. First, there are the twelve apostles, that group established by Jesus and, as we have seen, so easily and quickly phased out as a numerical identity. The twelve apostles are critically important, of course, both as a reality and a symbol. They are a kind of founding fathers, an apostolic college, the living witnesses to Jesus (the Christ Event). Therefore they are direct touchstones with his will and his ministry (see 1 Cor 15:5, Acts 6:1 ff, Rv 21:14). As long as they are around, they carry weight, the weight of keeping all others faithful to the Jesus tradition. But the New Testament writings and traditions show us others also called apostles who were not members of the original twelve. These are the wandering people who bring the message of the Good News to others, who minister to them and encourage them. They often overlap with the role of teacher and prophet. Saint Paul would be the classic example of the traveling apostle.

After these wandering apostles we find teachers and prophets who proclaimed the word of God, celebrated it in liturgical assembly, and gave inspired utterances. We also find widows who seem to be more than women with deceased husbands, but a kind of religious order whose members were of proven piety and character and who did works of hospitality (1 Tm 5:9-13). Deacons are mentioned as engaging in works of charity and "waiting on tables" (Acts 6:2) but who moved, as we have seen, into more activity, blurring with the travelling apostles, prophets, and teachers. In fact, they could be considered almost a new group of apostles as they helped found the various communities.

It was from just such a community at Antioch in Syria that Ananias was sent to heal Paul of his blindness. Then there are listed here and there healers, interpreters of tongues, administrators, and others (see 1 Cor 12:4-5, 28). There were, then, a variety of agents and officers who engaged in ministering to the small communities and house-churches of the first century. All arose as the needs of the community demanded. As might be expected, not all ministers were either adequate or worthy. Some could be quite divisive. The pastoral epistles (those written by Paul or another author in his style to Timothy and Titus bearing on practical, pastoral matters) were written to counteract the unworthy leader.

There are two other very important ministries that appear in the New Testament and the other writings as well. One is the person called the "guardian" of the community. That word translates as "bishop." The other term is "presbyter" and sometimes the terms of guardian and presbyter are used so interchangeably that it's hard to tell if and when there is a distinction. There is some significance to how often the New Testament writers are unclear in this whole matter of ministries. They appear to be casually imprecise, vague, and indefinite. And this, of course, indicates that the exact structure and definition of the various ministries were obviously not a pressing matter for them. But this is exactly as we might expect if, in fact, the early church is using that freedom from Jesus to evolve its ministries under the guidance of the Holy Spirit. On the other hand, what does come across strongly is that whatever the precise definition of ministry and office is, they must both be geared to community service (*diakonia*). Again, the community is shaping the ministry, not the other way around.

Getting back to the bishop (guardian) and the presbyter we must explore their origins. We will take the presbyter first. The word literally means elder. It is Jewish in expression but universal in theme. Whether they are bald, large-headed beings in Star Trek, bearded Merlins at Camelot, or those cigar box Dutch Masters of Holland, such advisors to the king or prince are usually older men, steeped in the ancient lore, full of wisdom, and noted for integrity of life. (There are always exceptions, as Susanna in the book of Daniel found out.) Such elders form an advisory council to the king, who at least listens to them, knowing that he ignores their advice at his own peril. (See 1 Kgs 12:6-16 for a classic example.) Such elders are a part of the history of Egypt, Babylon and Israel and all ancient peoples.

These elders were called presbyters. Israel's establishment of them goes back to Moses, whose father-in-law, perhaps thinking of his neglected daughter, urged Moses to get help "for the thing is too heavy for you ... choose able men from all the people ... and let them judge the people at all times" (Ex 18:18-22). In another tradition, Moses is directly approached by God who tells him to gather seventy elders "and I will take some of the spirit which is upon you and put it upon them" (Nm 11:16-18). (Note that God gives *some* of Moses' spirit away: he is still full leader and the others are subordinate to him.) These elders continued on and off during Israel's history. They are found as the king's council at the time of the monarchy and after the exile they are prominent in the rebuilding of the temple. Around the second century before Christ, the elders have devolved into a kind of senate. They become the Supreme Native Council of Jerusalem, the *synedrion* or the sanhedrin of our gospels.

The jurisdiction of this Jerusalem sanhedrin was technically limited to Jerusalem but there was some undefined authority beyond the city. We might recall, for example, that this sanhedrin sent letters to Damascus in Syria to apprehend any Christians there (Acts 9:2). Each territory in Palestine had its group of ruling elders or sanhedrin. Even after the year 70 when the temple was destroyed, the Jerusalem sanhedrin simply rerouted itself and formed a rabbinical academy.

We should note that these elder-presbyters (we'll use this hyphenated form for a while) from the beginning were "ordained," that is, they were installed in their position by the laying on of hands. They were not priests nor were they connected with the temple in any way. They were simply invested in their roles by the laying on of hands, which was an old symbol for the transference or bestowal of power. This Moses did for Joshua and he in turn to others. This the prophets did. The tasks of these elder-presbyters lay mainly in the role of judging, guiding, and in general, presiding over the local community.

Some of the elder-presbyters, collectively called the presbyterate,[4] were sent out to carry messages to various Jewish communities and promote piety and learning. They carried a certain air of authority coming as they did from the main Jerusalem sanhedrin. They could even raise funds and preside over the local courts (the very things the travelling Paul did). They were something like an ambassador or, in Catholic terms, an apostolic delegate. Such "sent members" had a special title derived from the word *sent:* apostle.

At the time of the Christian era, such Jewish elder-presbyters in their role as travelling apostles made the rounds with the power and authority of the great sanhedrin to redress wrongs, bring judgment, and form a liaison with the civil government. No one will fail to notice the parallel with the first Christian communities with *their* elder-presbyters at Jerusalem under the leadership of James (Acts 21:17—not the same as the apostle James) and the sent-out travelling apostles such as Paul and Barnabas. The parallel should surprise no one who remembers that all of the first Christians were Jews. As Jews they would instinctively follow their ancestral social forms. That is why they largely adopted the presbyterate model of ruling their first communities, especially, as we might surmise, in that very first Jewish community at Jerusalem.

There were then at Jerusalem a counterpart Christian sanhedrin, or presbyterate, composed of the apostles (the original) and the elder-presbyters. The latter were of course inferior to the original twelve apostle witnesses to Jesus (on that very account) and did not have the same status as the visiting teachers or prophets. Nevertheless they shared authority and decision making. Recall the opening lines of the letter sent out from the Council of Jerusalem: "The brethren, both the apostles and the presbyters, to the brethren who are of the Gentiles ..." (Acts 15:23). In the first years, then, when the church was small, confined mostly to loose communities of Jewish Christians and house meetings, this Jerusalem sanhedrin of Christian elder-presbyters was the final authority but always, of course, in connection with the original apostles of Jesus. The other church communities that sprung up outside Jerusalem naturally looked to them for approval, support, and supervision.

—4—

In due time, and here we begin our variety of tradition, not all communities beyond Jerusalem followed this pattern. For example, Barnabas is sent by the Jerusalem sanhedrin to Antioch in Syria which is a mixed congregation of Jewish and Gentile converts who have neither a resident apostle nor a temple. Instead, Barnabas winds up organizing the local community around local prophets or charismatic figures (Acts 13:1). These local leaders have no special title and were referred to by Paul simply as "those who labor for the community" or "those who are over you." Such prophets or charismatic figures were beholden to the travelling apostles who founded them.[5]

Other places of beginning Christians seemed to be ruled by local homogeneous councils, a kind of homebound elder system acting democratically in concert with no specific head. On the other hand, some communities had presbyter-councils but with a single person in charge as leader. In all cases, it seems, when the founding travelling apostles moved on, leadership was taken over by local leaders arising from the community (see 1 Thes 5:12). Beholden to the general overseeing of the apostles while they were alive (1 Cor 14:36, 37) and originating from local grass roots, they ruled in virtue of their charismatic gifts, or their position as prophets-teachers, or as persons put forth from the local council of rulers or elders, or as appointed directly by the people.

We get a hint of one kind of variety or other from Saint Paul. There were many abuses at the church in Corinth, a community founded by Paul. Yet in his strongly-worded letters to them, he never addresses himself to any particular leader or group of officials. This is somewhat strange since the abuses were really serious. It would seem, therefore, that Paul did not know who was in charge. If this is so, it would suggest that the people there appointed their own leaders or perhaps that the one in charge was an equal among equals in some kind of presbyterate.

In this case we have a democratic body ruling. Another alternative is that the people as a whole, in their variety of gifts, were responsible for faith and good order.[6] When we look at other New Testament writings beyond Paul's, we gather from 1 Peter and the johannine epistles that they had in their communities an independent council of elder-presbyters who were grouped, not around a travelling apostle like Paul, but around a stable, inresident president much like the Jerusalem Council gathered around the presidency of James.

This "presidency" is significant and brings us to our final office to be considered. We find it as a distinct development after Paul's death (and one which he would approve). Around the years 58 to 62 at Philippi and Ephesus among the ruling elder-presbyter body, one of their number begins to stand out as the leader. This is someone clearly "more equal" than the others even though he works with them. He is called the guardian or the bishop and he is assisted by his deacons. In the pastoral epistles, on the other hand, he appears to be someone quite distinct from the elder-presbyters.

We can only speculate that he simply emerged as leader, was appointed by one of the original twelve apostles, or was elected by the elder-presbyters or the community. In any case, his appearance gives us the third of the threefold positions of leadership and office that would become enshrined in the Christian tradition: bishop, presbyter, and deacon.

This office of bishop emerged unevenly into the prime leadership in the church. We will trace elsewhere how the bishop gradually came to dominate, and how the office eventually freed itself from any intricate association with the elder-presbyters. We will determine the approximate period when he winds up totally superior to them and they wind up as dependent extensions of him. We will even observe how this emerging, single monarchial ruler in the church absorbs some of the charisms of the other ministries. But what we want to see briefly now is what pushed him into such prominence.

It is not too simplistic to respond by saying that the office of bishop was propelled by the pressures of history. First of all, the original twelve apostles died. In normal times, perhaps the elder-presbyters could handle things as well and continue the leadership in the church. In Rome this rule by elder-presbyters seems, in fact, to be the case. But then fierce pressures descended on the church. There were rending heresies for one thing. Persecution would take its toll in both deaths and defections. The expected second coming of Christ was apparently being delayed. With all of these factors, there was felt a dire need to retrench, to dig in for the long haul. Survival was at stake. There was a desperate need for direction, for a living rule of faith, a living guide of what was right and wrong. There was a need to preserve the genuine apostolic tradition. In a word, there was need to centralize.

To all of these needs the early church responded with two basic reactions. One was the writing down of the normative Jesus story, with all of its variety of interpretations and traditions, and this is what we call our normative New Testament. The second reaction was to turn to a centralized source of leadership. The emerging guardian-bishop was just the one for this. Crises had assured his ascending and firm position.

We leave our consideration of the bishop for the moment and close with two comments. The first one concerns apostolic succession. Our usual understanding is that Jesus passed on his authority and power to the twelve apostles and in turn, before they died, they passed it on to others, and these others to still more until the present time. The imagery that comes across is a physical one: a direct hand-to-hand, person-to-person contact, like the marathon runners passing on the torch.

Actually, apostolic succession refers to the whole apostolic tradition. It is this "deposit of faith" that gets passed on, and naturally care and fidelity are paramount. This need not and does not imply any physical passing on to a particular person. It implies rather that to the church at large, through whatever mechanism, this tradition must be handed on. It need not be through the apostles by way of individual hand-to-hand process from them to the bishops. It does mean that it is through the apostles to the church as a whole, in whatever way the church institutionalizes the routine, whether through bishops or elder-presbyters or gifted members or living congregations.

What is critical, in other words, is not the person-to-person contact, but the apostolic witness—the living church connection. The bishops wind up as the most visible (and perhaps the best) keepers of the tradition in the light of the history we have seen. They are indeed the "successors of the apostles" in this sense. But there is no intrinsic necessity that they are exclusively the bearers of tradition, for we have seen that other forms existed in the primitive church. At the same time, there is every reason to see the church as the fundamental receiver of the apostolic witness and, as we said, through whatever mechanism the Spirit empowers.

The second comment is that we have been using the terms *ministry* and *office* somewhat interchangeably. Basically they are the same. Ministry serves the mission of the church and refers to the service of the community that keeps the gospel alive and the tradition intact. Office refers to leadership in the community. The trouble is that for a very long time all the ministries were absorbed into the clerical office and so no distinctions were made. Nowadays, as ministries are being detached from the clerical office and redistributed among the people, the two terms of ministry and office are sometimes thought to be opposed. We must remember, however, that the early church saw no such opposition. Rather it saw office as a ministerial charism that was institutionalized. It saw office, too, as a gift of the Spirit and as such an expression of ministry.

So far, then, we have seen this much. There was a variety of ministries in the early church from prophets to widows. There was a variety of ways to rule—from the original twelve to the presbyterate (with a leader or without one) to the gifted charismatic leader to the guardian-bishop. How they changed, developed, disappeared, coalesced, and got absorbed is the story of the succeeding chapters. Meanwhile it is well to be reminded from our brief survey regarding these many varieties of ministries and the several ways of presiding over the Christian community that "we can go on to say that there is no evidence in the New Testament that any one individual exercised all these functions in the first century of the Christian era."[7] A variety of ministries was still the norm.

CHAPTER TWO

From Prophet To Presbyter To Priest

—1—

In the first century around the Mediterranean Sea we have not only a pluralism of Jesus traditions, but a variety of ministries and overseeing as well. The epistle of James, for example, tells us that the elder-presbyter church order was in vogue. We all remember the well-known passage concerning the anointing of the sick: "Is there anyone sick among you? Let him call in the presbyters of the church ...." The johannine communities started out as spontaneous charismatic communities but wound up with authoritative leaders, although with the insistence that the real minister is Christ and his Spirit. Matthew's gospel reflects a church community, perhaps in Syria, that still seems to be under the individual prophets' and teachers' leadership, and they do not seem to be aware of the elder-presbyters model.

In general, the Roman sources speak of elder-presbyters who seem to be appointed for life, have cultic functions, and preside over the community. The Asian churches seem to have bishops surrounded by an elder-presbyter council of advisors. Whatever the variety, as we indicated in the last chapter, there is a distinct trend, in the face of heresy and the need to pass on the apostolic tradition intact, to depend less and less on charismatic prophets, teachers, and wandering apostles and more and more on stable, resident bishops. Even when it comes to the term *bishop* itself, it seems to be a truism that the term is one favored by the Gentile churches (Phil 1:1) whereas *elder* is the term preferred on Palestinian soil. Needless to say, we really do not know how the bishops were chosen anymore than we know whether there were presbyters in the seven churches of the Apocalypse. Even here, in this exotic book, the ascribing of a royal power to the faithful in general (Rv 1:6, 3:31) no more excludes the presence of elder-presbyters, or even of a bishop for that matter, than it did in 1 Peter (see 2:9, 5:1). Precision, in short, is not to be had.

This untidy and confusing but obvious development of ministries and office is evident also in contemporary writings outside the New Testament. For instance, the letter of Clement of Rome tells us that Antioch was still in the old pauline tradition of having a presbyterate dependent on a distant apostle. In this case the distant apostle is Clement himself who from Rome freely butts into affairs at Antioch. We are not sure whether Clement himself was the bishop of Rome or the president of its presbyterate. An educated guess is that he was both. On the other hand, we also discover that the travelling apostle-teacher-prophet is around (sometimes all three charisms are invested in one person, other times among several). Then again, *Didache* speaks of two classes of church office: the bishop and his deacons, and the prophets and teachers. The first are appointed, the latter arise from charisms given by the Spirit.

At this point in church history (early second century) we notice too that the charismatic prophets and teachers are still more highly thought of than the bishops and deacons. That is why the *Didache* (15, 2) cautions that the latter ought not to be slighted in any way at the expense of the former. Maybe it was the still remaining high fervor and expectation of Jesus' second coming that were factors in the popularity of the prophets and teachers and made people prefer them to settled-down office holders. On the other hand, when Jesus did not come again as immediately as expected, then the charismatic prophet-teacher would wane and the settled-down office holder would ascend.

By the time we meet a writer like Ignatius of Antioch (d. 117) and his disciple Polycarp, and some decades later Irenaeus of

Lyons (d.c. 202) we have the end product of what was begun in the pastoral epistles: the centrality and triumph of a strong monarchial bishop. Older patterns remain and ruling by the elders-presbyters is still common, so much so that the terms *bishop* and *presbyter* are still being used interchangeably. Nevertheless change is being made. The office of bishop as chief presbyter *over all the others* is growing. His leadership is being entrenched and soon he will subordinate the ruling presbyterate.

The controlling concern, as we indicated before, seems to be stability. Wandering apostles, charismatic prophets and teachers, once the darlings of the first communities, were frankly becoming a liability for the church of the long haul. In fact, they were more of a disturbance since they were by definition not subject to control. We sense even as early as Saint Paul's letters the need to calm down too much enthusiasm. The *Didache* is at a position of saying that wandering prophets were indeed welcomed into the communities— for a day's visit. After a day, they should leave. If they stayed more than three days, this is taken as a sign that they are false prophets! Perhaps we can also sense an apologetic transitional note as the author of the *Didache* tries to sell the bishop and deacon: "Accordingly elect for yourselves bishops and deacons ... for they too render your the service of prophets and teachers. Do not despise them; after all they are your dignitaries together with the prophets and teachers" (15, 1, 2).

Again, we must sense what is happening here. The church is bracing itself against the sinfulness of its own members, heresies, the growing numbers of converts, persecution, the death of the original twelve, and the delay of the second coming. The church is settling down into history. There is less interest in the charismatic and more interest in stability. Charismatic people, sociologically speaking, must somehow be brought under control by the office of the bishop. As one scholar puts it, "From the saying 'The church is where the Spirit is,' the struggle with gnosticsm led to the new thesis: the church is where the bishop is .... The Spirit reveals himself now, not as formerly in prophets and those who spoke in tongues, but in the bishop and clergy whom the bishop led ...."[1] What eventually happened was that the charismatic ministers were not so much suppressed as institutionalized, not so much rejected as merged into office. The bishop absorbed the role of prophet and teacher. By the beginning of the third century, he is holding local synods or conferences. By the end of the third century, it is clear that he has full authority in church life.

Yet we must repeat here that in the process our ancestors did not make sharp and conscious separation between the charismatic ministries and the office of the bishop, as if the two were opposed. They did not look on it that way. On the contrary, they had other bishops lay hands on a new bishop as an outward sign of communicating to him the gift of the Spirit which Jesus received from his Father and passed on to his apostles. The ordination prayers and the fellow bishops' action make it clear that even in his structured office the bishop *is* charismatic and not a usurper who "took over" from charismatic figures. He assumes or is given the role, not preempts it.[2] The theory is sound. Nevertheless in practice there is no denying that there has historically been a gathering into one person and his office what were formerly the gifts of many.

The theory goes astray, of course, when it translates to mean that only ordination gives competence, authority, and the right of professional governance. It goes further astray when eventually all jurisdictional and administrative powers in the church come to be seen as an extension of the sacramental powers conferred at ordination. In short, there is a movement here away from the more pristine collaborative and mutual ministries of the New Testament.

Meanwhile, to return to our current interest, what is happening to the ruling elder-presbyters? They remain as advisors to the bishop for the time being and then gradually devolve into mere honorary figures as the deacons become the more powerful ones in the bishops' retinue. The deacons, originally intended to serve the community, now serve the bishop. They are his eyes and ears and personal emissaries. In this role, they become quite powerful (for they also hold the purse strings) and arouse the jealousy of the presbyters. The Council of Nicea in 325 has some harsh words for those deacons who have become too haughty and overbearing, even having the effrontery to sit higher than the presbyters at the liturgy and receive communion before them. By a twist of history, however, the elder-presbyters soon will get their revenge. The deacons will go into decline until revived centuries later by the Council of Vatican II.

Meanwhile, in our discussion of the various forms of

ministry—bishop, presbyter, deacon, widows, prophets, healers, teachers, and the like—we have a question. Does this exhaust our list? It does. But there is perhaps an uneasiness. Something is missing. So, another question. Where is the word *priest* in the New Testament? The answer: nowhere.

—2—

We usually associate the word priest with ritual, cult, sacrifice and altar, whether we're thinking of the Catholic priest or some ancient priestly figure wielding his sacrificial knife over some animal or human victim. Yet the curious thing is that when we take a look at the New Testament testimony, we find almost total silence about ritual, cult, and sacrifice. We discover, in fact, an almost cultless Christianity. And this is all the more striking when we consider how highly cultic contemporary Jewish life was and that the early Christians were not only all Jews but that they initially associated themselves with the temple (Acts 2:46). True, we do read of baptism and the eucharist in the New Testament but they come off rather tamely and sparse in structure and performance. There is simply no high ritual in early Christianity and certainly no such term as priest is ever applied to any Christian individual, including the twelve apostles.

Furthermore, Christianity broke from its pagan and Jewish predecessors by having no concept of a sacred place where God could be encountered. Jesus made a clear statement to the Samaritan woman that neither on her so-called sacred mountain nor in Jerusalem would God be worshipped. Rather he would be worshipped interiorly in spirit and truth by genuine worshippers (Jn 4:20-24) and that where two or three would be gathered in his name, he would be in their midst (Mt 18:20). Furthermore, although Jesus certainly prayed himself and urged prayer on his followers, he seems quite critical of all cultic acts (Mk 12:28-34; Jn 2:14-22; Jn 4:21-24). For Jesus, the whole world is his Father's domain and obedience to God's word is worth more than any sacrifices. He also took a dim view of the Jewish dietary laws, used David as an example for eating the sacred bread reserved only to the priests, was cavalier about the Sabbath and, of course, was condemned to death on the charge that he blasphemed against the temple, that great symbol of institutionalized Judaism.

Early tradition follows Jesus by urging believers to be "living stones" in a spiritual house, offering up spiritual sacrifices to God through Jesus (1 Pt 2:4). Therefore, they are not to build temples as *the* place for the residence of the diety, but rather buildings as gathering places for believers who are the church. The bottom line is that since there are to be no sacred places there are to be, in this sense, no specially sacred persons such as priests to mediate the divine.

As a result of all this, the New Testament goes out of its way to avoid the term priest so there would be no confusion about the message of Jesus and also no confusion with either the pagan or Jewish priests, temples, or caste distinction. Notice, therefore, that with all his lists of the various gifts and offices, Paul never uses the word priest and, as we said, nowhere in the entire New Testament is it used of a Christian individual. But, of course, the word *is* used and where it is, it is applied to Jesus. The source, almost entirely, is in the epistle to the Hebrews. Yet, even here, Jesus is called a priest in a very special use of the term, for we must remember that, in his contemporary society, Jesus was not a traditional priest. He was of the wrong tribe for one thing, although some have tried to get him in on either the Aaronic or Levitical lines through the juggling of the various genealogies presented in Matthew and Luke's gospels.[3] Jesus was considered to be a Jewish layman, a rabbi, a teacher, but that's all. Therefore, in Hebrews, he is not a Levitical priest or one in the ancient line of Aaron or Zadoc but in the strange line of Melchizedek, that man of no genealogy.

What is even more startling as one reads Hebrews is the distinct impression that sacrificial cult is not a fitting thing for Christianity anyway, since what Jesus did is unique, "once and for all," and cannot be added to or repeated. The author of Hebrews is out to impress on the community of believers that they had to abandon the purely cultic sphere and belong exclusively to the Lord. What Jesus did was to supersede all Jewish precedent and preempted all subsequent expressions (not, however, as we shall see, sign or sacramental expressions of the unrepeatable act on Calvary). As Bernard Cooke writes,

So strong are the statements of Hebrews on the absolute uniqueness of Christ's priestly act that it is in a class by itself, that it is all-sufficient in its salvific power, and that its culmination in the heavenly liturgy is a lasting reality, that no room remains for anything we might call cultic priestly activity on the part of Christians. And it seems that this is the way the church in the early decades thought: there is no place for *hiereis* [priests] in the church (or any place for that matter) since there is one abiding *hiereus* [priest] ... What is clear is that no official of the early church, not even one of the twelve, was looked upon as a cultic priest who offered sacrifices.[4]

We have already taken note that Paul's type of church communities was more charismatic and those of Acts more Jewish with its elder-presbyter ruling format. In either case, office in them was based on teaching and preaching and overseeing, not on any sacred theme.

For all these reasons, the early Christians avoided the term priest. The emphasis rather was on the building up of the community of believers by the leaders. Such leaders were not seen in any way as intermediaries for the simple reason that "there is one God and there is one mediator between God and men, the man Christ Jesus who gave himself up as a ransom for all" (1 Tm 2:5, 6). Rather such leaders were to be seen as "stewards of the mysteries of God" (1 Cor 4:1) arousing the faith of a priestly people. There was no longer any distinctions between the sacred and the profane. God is not confined to his temple but is available to all in Christ, who is with his people until the end of the world. All the baptized people are sanctified. They are all priestly, "a holy people, a royal priesthood" (1 Pt 1:2). Priestliness, the offering up of sanctified lives and works to the Father, is not confined to any one *individual*. There is to be no compromise to the universal accessibility of the Lord. No one is excluded nor is anyone given special status in the community of Jesus because the Spirit is poured out upon all as St. Peter reminded his audience on the first Pentecost. The Spirit, it is revealed, is radically democratic (Acts 2:17).

Yet, with all of this background, we wind up by the fourth century with a fairly defined (and confined) concept of priest as applied to an individual Christian. How did this happen? Or perhaps, for us with our modern minds, this question of the priest is intimately tied in with another one whose answer might satisfy us on all points: we know that all this time the eucharist was being celebrated. Who did it? Or, again, as we would phrase it, "Who said Mass?"

—3—

Actually we must reroute the question "Who said Mass?" to its more precise form, namely, "Who presided at the eucharist?" This is not a matter of wording or semantics. The rephrased question, as we shall see, hits at the heart of the matter. But, first, let us give a quick and direct answer as to who presided at the eucharist. The New Testament gives surprisingly few allusions to eucharistic celebrations, but what allusions there are indicate that it is the prophets and teachers who in fact preside at the eucharist, (Acts 13:1-2), those people mentioned by Saint Paul after the apostles (1 Cor 12:28).

Our first century document, the *Didache,* backs this up. It indicates that it is precisely those prophets who "pronounce the blessing at the eucharist" and even have enough charism to make up their own prayers. Furthermore, as we saw, if such prophet-teachers are overworked, then bishops and deacons can then preside. But it is interesting to note why: not because they are bishops or deacons as such but because "they too fulfill among you the office of the prophets and teachers. Do not hold them in contempt; for they count as honorable men among you" (14, 1:15, 2). In other words, community leadership entitled one to preside at the eucharist.

The letters of Clement of Rome inform us that presiders of the eucharist are not only bishops and presbyters, but "other eminent men with the consent of the whole church" (44, 3). Tertullian (d.c. 220) held the singular opinion that even a layman could preside in the absence of the ordained priest (*Exhort. Cast.* 7, 3). The work known as the *Apostolic Witness of Hippolytus* talks about confessors presiding at the eucharist. Confessors were the almost-martyrs, those imprisoned, tortured, and nearly killed for the faith (those who "confessed" the faith in extreme witness). In primitive, popular Christianity, their bravery and endurance qualified them as teachers and prophets, natural leaders, and therefore ones entitled to preside at the eucharist.

We have a record that during the persecution of Decius, an elder-presbyter from Carthage could take it upon himself to preside at the eucharist without the knowledge or permission of the bishop. According to the Council of Arles held in 314, in the absence of priests, deacons may preside at the eucharist in an emergency during the persecution of Diocletian. While some of us are catching our breath in surprise at this revelation so different from what we were brought up to believe, (namely, saying Mass being the divinely exclusive prerogative of the priest) we must not lose sight of an important principle that has emerged here. That principle is that, in the minds of the first century Christians, what really entitled one to preside at the eucharist was his role in presiding over the community. The two are intimately connected. Saints Justin (d. 165) and Irenaeus (d.c. 202) also hold that the one who presides over the life of the community should preside over its eucharist. Again, a rather constant principle is operating. The liturgical leader was not only the bishop. There was simply no notion at first of somebody as an especially designated minister to make Christ present in the eucharist.

Behind that ancient New Testament principle that the one who presides over the community presides at the eucharist is a compelling logic. After all, to preside basically means to "gather into one," to build up the body of Christ. The whole concept of gathering, unifying, encouraging, and protecting that is implied in presidency necessarily finds its highest expression in the eucharist, *the* celebration of unity and service and fellowship. It was only fitting, therefore, that the one who is president of the community should be president of the eucharist. It was only natural, for instance, that the bishop's ancient ordination ritual should speak of his liturgical presidency as the logical outcome of his role as community leader.

> This ... strengthens the hypothesis according to which one presided at the Eucharist in the pre-Nicene Church because one presided over the church ... if we summarize the testimonies of the pre-Nicene church, a general perspective emerges. The bond between the apostles and presidents of the Eucharist is to be found only with

Clement and secondarily with Hippolytus. The perception of the president of the Eucharist as an explicit sacerdotal figure is not attested to before the beginning of the third century.... On the other hand, with all of the witnesses we note that it is a fact, and most often it is axiomatic (Clement, Ignatius, Justin, Tertullian, Hippolytus, Cyprian and the canonical tradition deriving from Hippolytus) that those who preside over the life of the church preside at the eucharist.[5]

It is interesting therefore to note (1) the diversity of presiders at the eucharist in the early centuries, and (2) that such presidency was not tied in with any personal power of the individual or personal "priestly" characteristics, but tied in with community presidence. This ancient practice could have profound influence in our day. But more of this later.

There is another perspective to notice concerning the bishop or whoever "presides" at the eucharist. It is not said that he offers gifts. Rather the whole church does this. He is merely the president of an assembly which is the real offerer of the gifts at worship— another expression of the priesthood of the faithful. Once more, "presidency at the eucharist assembly is seen as the liturgical, prophetic and mystic dimension of the pastoral charge of building up the Church which is conferred in ordination."[6] Thus ordination, as it appears in the ancient texts, is fundamentally oriented toward one's pastoral role, one of the critical parts of which is to preside at the community's eucharist. One is ordained to build and celebrate community, and flowing from this, to preside at the eucharist. It is not the other way around, as most of us have learned. One is not ordained to preside at the eucharist and *then,* as a side effect, preside over the community. That is why ancient canons voided the ordination of anyone who was a free-floating presider of the eucharist without a community. Such was a contradiction. As we ponder this, we can see there is something wrong in our system of having some strange priest sent to a community he does not know, even though our Catholic tradition, unlike the Protestant one, puts the emphasis on "being sent" rather than on "being called" (by the community). This may not be a moot question in our highly mobile society where community is hard come by anyway. Still, it is interesting to see the ancient point of view.

—4—

With the variety of "celebrants" or "presiders," we still have to meet the term *priest* as we understand it in our modern sense. The beginnings go way back. It is in the letters of Clement of Rome (d.c. 97) that we begin to find a language that would eventually give us a foundation to use the word, priest. Clement begins to see parallels between the Christian martyr and the ancient priesthood of Aaron. (Remember that Judaism had a high priest and priestly levites who served at the temple.) Clement sees an analogy here in the two offerings of life, the martyr and the old animal sacrifice. While using sacrificial language he does not yet use the term priest of any specific ministry but he is setting the stage for another day. (This is the Clement who, as far as we know, first uses the term laity as does his contemporary, Ignatius of Antioch—note that another seed is planted.) The *Didache* adds to the impetus when it also uses Old Testament terminology in describing the eucharist as a sacrifice and the author does use the term high priest to describe the visiting prophets. We are still in the realm of analogy here, but we can see how such analogies could and would grow.

This dipping into the Old Testament for symbols and language was an old Christian thing to do. The gospels, especially Matthew's, are full of such allusions. Yet, on the other hand, there was a deliberate move to separate from Judaism, not by denying it as root and matrix, but by claiming to be its legitimate flowering. And, as far as is the flower from its roots, so did Christianity move from Judaism. What we are saying is that there is a serious tension in the beginning with the need to claim Judaism and at the same time "grow away" from it. It is this bouncing back between these two poles that is going to give us the dominant theme of priesthood in Catholicism. Let's take a look.

We said that the Christian community considered itself the continuation and fulfillment of Israel. The Christians were now God's certified chosen people (1 Pt 2:10) since Jesus of Nazareth is the Messiah of Israel. Paul would insist that through baptism one became a part of God's people and as such a true child of Abraham (Gal 3) and that someday, Jews and Gentiles were, in fact, to form one common humanity (Eph 2:11-18). Christianity was really Israel brought to completion. "And if you are Christ's then you are Abraham's offspring, heirs according to the promise" (Gal 3:29). So wrote Paul. In Romans he speaks of a kind of transfer of Israel's prerogatives to the church (9-11).

The author of Hebrews takes Old Testament figures and symbols and applies them to Christ. The gospels themselves are already in the process of replacement. Recall that Luke has the risen Christ apply the Old Testament to himself: "Beginning with Moses and all the prophets [he] interpreted to them in all the scriptures the things concerning him" (Lk 24:27). (We must remember that as yet there were no Christian scriptures and so scriptures in the New Testament always mean what we call the Old Testament or the Hebrew scriptures.) In a word, it was common early teaching that Judaism had had its day and the one who was foretold in the Hebrew scriptures had come in Christ.[7]

Because of this fulfillment and replacement concept, there was at first a really radical separation in practice and thought from Judaism, if not from its social forms. Christianity quickly broke with Jewish religious cult, its many detailed observances, and the guidance of the Jewish priesthood which by now had absorbed much of the governing role of the old defunct kingship. Most of all, as Paul made abundantly clear, it broke with the Law. There is no desire to fill in the gap. There is no inclination to bring in any kind of priestly mediation that was such a part of the first Christians' Judaism. This is even more remarkable when we consider that, according to Luke, a fair number of Jewish priests were converts (Acts 6:7). For the first Christians then there is no king, no priest from their past. The prophet is kept on as a heritage and even here he (or she) appears not in any institutional form (as yet unabsorbed into the bishopric) but in a spontaneous, charismatic form.[8] And the teacher was kept on, that critically important unifier of the people who did yeoman service in the new faith. Otherwise, all that the early Christians seem to have picked up from their Jewish past was the system of the elder-presbyter rule which, even in Judaism, was never considered to be divinely inspired.

At this point another intriguing perspective must be introduced. We have really so little information about the centuries immediately before Jesus, about the kind of Judaism that existed.

Recent scholarship has, however, shed much light on one critical phenomenon that occurred then, the rise of the Pharisees. The Pharisees are usually seen as the heavies in the New Testament (reflecting current hostilities between them and the congregation; of the gospel writers) but, in fact, it seems that the whole pharisaic movement constituted a vital and powerful impact in pre-Christian Judaism. As such, it strongly affected and shaped the Christian church and its whole concept of ministry. Perhaps its main impact on Christianity was the emergence of a new religious figure who was neither prophet nor priest. This was the scribe, who was later called the rabbi. The radical change was that the rabbi was not a cultic figure, not connected with the traditional priesthood. Rather, he was a combination of everyday interpreter of the Law and an "in-the-field" minister of mercy, healing, and good works. His domain was equally the synagogue and the market place. He not only explained and applied the Law to daily, practical situations for everyday people, but he lived and moved among them as a kind of Mother Teresa figure. In due time it was this rabbi, this non-cultic figure, who replaced the priest as the main symbol of Jewish religious commitment. He was the one who was "ordained" in that he was publicly selected and proclaimed by the community.

Now it was this new form of the rabbinate, the academic field man that Jesus knew, which therefore formed the basis of his own ministry. Even a casual reading of the New Testament shows that Jesus was rabbi—and called so—in this classical sense. He interpreted the Law for everyday people and was in the field as a man showing mercy, healing, and good works. Consistent with his pharisaical background, Jesus also affirmed the primacy of the public ministry over the cultic priesthood in the daily life of the church. This was a major shift, prepared by pharisaic Judaism, and this is the attitude and practice which, as we have seen, the early church inherited. Early Christianity was clearly one of interpretation and service, not of cult and priesthood. Even Jesus' presiding at the Last Supper was done more in his natural role as head of a pharisaic brotherhood than as a priest as understood in his own day. Peter, Paul, and the rest followed this model.

We mention this background to demonstrate how radically separated the early Christians were from Judaism and therefore how surprising was their dramatic reversal. The Christians did not return to pre-pharisaic Judaism in all ways and not directly, but obliquely and by borrowing terms to be used in a new and analogous way. The regression comes in the way the later Christian church picked up terms, customs, and rituals it once neglected. As we saw, early writers like Hippolytus begin to use Old Testament priestly terms for eucharistic presiders. For instance, he calls the bishop a high priest (though not at this time the presbyter), and gives us the first written ordination ceremony for bishop, presbyter, and deacon. Cyprian used priestly vocabulary in talking about bishops and is also the first one to use the phrase "other Christ" in speaking about the bishop presiding at the eucharist (a term developed in a highly dubious way in medieval times; even Vatican II would not use it). Still, we ought to note the old principle at work in Cyprian. His whole emphasis on the bishop is that of the unifying head of the community. If the bishop presides at the eucharist, he does so precisely in view of his role as the guarantor of unity.

But the real movement toward adopting pre-pharisaic priestly terminology came as a result of thinking about the eucharist itself. Old Testament categories of sacrifice began to be applied to it. As a result, the eucharistic celebration becomes very cultic (as distinct from the brotherhood meal presided over by the rabbi) and an elaborate liturgy is spun around it. Becoming more cultic, the eucharist demands, not a presider, but a priest—and here is where we get the connection. With the notion of sacrifice prevailing, then logically the place where the eucharistic meal takes place becomes á temple, the table becomes an altar, and the bishop becomes both high priest plus something dramatically more: he becomes a mediator between God and the human race in spite of Paul's words to Timothy that there is only one such mediator. All this, to be sure, is happening slowly but surely, so that by the third and fourth centuries we do have an entrenched word, priest, and it is attached to an individual Christian minister, namely, the bishop and to him only.

Why the later church returned to the pre-pharisaic days of Judaism with its heavy emphasis on the cultic priesthood we don't know; we can only guess. Perhaps it was Christianity's rapid movement to a gentile world, which was anti-semitic and so would not accept its current forms. Also, such gentiles would have little or no contact with the pharisaic Judaism out of which Jesus and his apostles came. On the other hand, they were familiar with sacrifices and their pagan priests were familiar symbols of power. Whatever the reason, once the connection between Christianity and old Judaism got started, it rapidly solidified throughout the ages to this present day. As Yves Congar has described the problem:

> Thus the first priestly act is the ministry of the Word. We have grown a bit forgetful of that fact. The Middle Ages understood our priesthood as founded in Aaron and therefore linked it to the cultic-ritualistic priesthood of the Old Testament; then it defined this very same priesthood by the power to celebrate the eucharist. Next the French school of the seventeenth centure (Berulle, Condren, Olier), which is the main source of the teaching given in seminaries and religious congregations, defined the priest as a religious and as an adorer of God. From all that there resulted a mainly cultic notion of the priesthood: we are priests to offer Mass. Is not that what the ordination ritual says?[9]

There is one more development, namely, how the title priest got transferred from the bishop to the priest we know today. It happened this way. Christianity grew rapidly and the bishops, always city people until the present time, could no longer oversee the far-flung communities springing up here and there, especially in the countryside. At one stage, they experimented with a kind of pro-bishop or delegate bishop in some districts but this did not work out. They might have looked to their deacons but by this time this was not feasible. The deacons had become too valuable and necessary as part of their staff. So the bishops turned to the elder-presbyters, or simply now, the presbyters. This was natural, as they were already overseeing local communities. They had begun already to do what the bishop did, especially in cases of emergency: they were doing the first part of Christian initiation, what we call baptism (the other part splitting off into what we call confirmation and still reserved to the bishop in the West—not in the East, however, where presbyters do the whole thing). Why not—according to our old principle that he who presides at community should preside at eucharist—why not have him preside at the eucharist, too? The bishops then simply delegated the presbyters to do this, without any special ordination at the time. The presbyter in turn received the new title of priest. As presbyter-priest, he was the bishop's delegate as he is to this day. There are many small symbols of this superior-delegated relationship such as the bishop's prerogative to bless all the oils used in local parishes on Holy Thursday or Passion Sunday. (In this way, he literally and figuratively keeps his finger in the local congregation.)

Now we have the distinctive triad of bishop, priest, and deacon and by the fourth century, talk of sacrifice and priest was quite common. As time went on, the parish priest took over more and more of the bishop's tasks on the local level. He became his clone and so, really, not that much different except for certain legal and canonical restrictions. Most theologians hold that there is no fundamental difference between a bishop and priest and in emergencies no power distinguishes them.

The practical separation of the priest's ministry from that of bishop is clearly marked off in the fourth century at the Council of Laodicea which decreed (canon 57) that there must not be bishops in the countryside, only priests, because the bishops were needed in the large city centers. In 341, the Councils of Sardica and Antioch said the same thing. Moreover, since the bishop did tend to keep the anointing part of baptism (confirmation), the power of reconciliation (penance), jurisdiction (king's role), and teaching (prophet's role) to himself, the priest by default became more and more identified principally as the minister of the eucharist, the one area left to him. In a word, what we have come to see as Jesus' threefold role of priest, prophet, and king, only the first was really left as the identifying mark of the newly endowed presbyter-priest.[10]

As we come to the end of this chapter, we might note that all this development also received an impetus from the slow demise of paganism. After all, paganism had its cults, mysteries, and priests. As these lost ground to Christianity, there was an almost psychological need for replacement, much perhaps like that felt by the first Jewish Christians after the destruction of the temple. In any case, either from pagan or Jewish sources, there was a distinct development in the Christian church: bishops did become high priests, presbyters became priests, the deacons became levites (on the way to the priesthood), the eucharistic banquet became a sacrifice, the table became an altar, and the Holy of Holies became the sanctuary. A strongly developed ritual of gesture began to overshadow the position and preaching of the word. The priest, by his special clothes and other privileges, began to be looked upon as a truly sacred personage whose main skills lay in liturgical rites and mediatorship, not in presiding over the communities' daily life.

Along with the increasing liturgy with its allegorical comparisons with ancient rites and its use of scriptural figures and symbols, there is a gradual decrease in catechetical instruction as infant baptism grows and adult converts from paganism decline. Moreover, doctrinal homiletics diminish after the age of the great heresies and public penance is reduced with the increasing reconciliation by monks. Gradually the Christian priest becomes more of a cultic functionary in his local sanctuary and less of a teacher, judge and minister of the word.[11]

So this is where priests come from, in our modern understanding of the term. The Catholic priests of today are yesterday's Jewish elder-presbyters who inherited the bishop's altar-presiding role when the bishops got too busy to take care of the outlying districts. In turn, the bishop's altar-presiding role came about when he absorbed the offices of prophet and teacher and others who used to preside at the eucharist in virtue of their community presidency. At the same time, the whole thing got started when the eucharist came to be seen in terms of sacrifice, thereby requiring the correlatives of sacrifice: altar, ritual, and priesthood. If you want to work it backwards, it reads like this: from sacrifice, to eucharist, to ritual, to altar, to priesthood, to presider—plus, in due time, the bishop who delegated the whole package to the presbyter who became known as the priest.

Meanwhile, we should prepare for the inevitable: for the bishops and priests so caught in this evolution, their role moves from service to status. And this is going to have profound ramifications in such major areas as celibacy, social divisions, authority, ordination, the priesthood of the faithful, ministry, especially the ministry of women, and the role of the modern priest.

CHAPTER THREE

From Priest To Power

—1—

We have seen how the former elder-presbyter has become the elder-priest, or simply priest. The priest has been given the powers of the bishop and has become in effect the bishop himself of his local parish community. We should not lose sight, however, of the old principle buried there, that it was precisely because the presbyter was already presider over the community that he qualified to preside at the eucharist. This connection got shaken loose in the course of history, however, and this is what we want to explore in this section.

For a long time this connection held firm. In fact, so strong was it that a major council of the church, the Council of Chalcedon in the fourth century, issued a law (canon 6) which forbade anyone to be ordained absolutely, that is, just for ordination's sake, without a community. This meant that no one was to be ordained unless he was attached to some kind of a community, whether a parish church, a chapel, or a monastery.

The ordination of a person not attached to a community was considered to be invalid, or at least without effect because the cleric would be in permanent suspension. To quote the canon:

Neither presbyter, deacon, nor any of the ecclesiastical order shall be ordained at large, not unless the person ordained is particularly ap-

45

pointed to a church in a city or village, or to a martyry [a chapel raised over a martyr's grave], or to a monastery. And if any have been ordained without a charge, the holy Synod decrees, to the reproach of the ordainer, that such an ordination shall be inoperative, and that such shall nowhere be suffered to officiate.

Yet in succeeding centuries, a change was made, a rather radical one with profound implications. In the twelfth century, the Third Lateran Council made a shift of emphasis and said that a man should not be ordained unless he was assured of a proper living. This seems to mean that he ought to have a community to support him which is not quite the same as having a community from the beginning from which he arose and which called him to service or accepted him. Pope Innocent I, who lived in the early fifth century, went further and said that someone could be ordained without a community (absolutely) if at least his bishop would financially provide for him. This meant he could free float as long as he had a "sponsor" or it meant that a man could apply to a bishop, get his backing and be sent where the bishop desired, not necessarily to his own community from which he came. This shift is subtle, but it implies that ordination, which formerly was tied in to the presidency of the local community, is altered to impart a personal investment of power that the individual could carry with him anywhere in his own person. What we are seeing here is a movement from delegation to a place, to acquisition of power for the person, *regardless* of community and place. Ordination has lost its communal rootedness and received a new twist, that of giving personal power.

The nature of this personal power became clarified in the thirteenth century at the Fourth Lateran Council. This council decreed that the eucharist could be celebrated only by a priest who has been validly ordained. Again, we should sense the critical shift. Ordination was always centered on community and was a response to it, its need for leadership, its need for eucharistic presidency, its need to recognize its gifted leaders. Now ordination is abstracted from all of this. It becomes a ritual for transferring private power, independent of community. The priest, wherever he goes in the world, has the individual power to change bread and wine into the body and blood of Christ and to forgive sins. With such awesome personal power, he has indeed arrived at the status of sacred person. Later on, the theological notion of the "character" would confirm the priest as intrinsically holy. That is, just by being ordained, by receiving the "mark," he becomes a man apart. His power is forever and follows him wherever he goes—with or without a community. He was now ordained absolutely. He could even finally do that totally inconceivable thing in the minds of the early Christians: he could celebrate a private Mass with no people present at all. Why not? He had all power in himself; he spoke the sanctifying intention. The people basically contributed nothing. All has gone half-circle. The community-oriented recognition of ordination becomes, in effect, private personal power to celebrate Mass.

Perhaps this should have been expected, for there has been a long history preceding such an outcome. This history starts early with the upward spiralling of the bishop's role. Bishops were not only heads of a single community but of several (to form a diocese). By the third century, they were wearing distinctive dress, even though Saint Ambrose of the fifth century still maintained that his distinctive dress was a life of integrity and holiness. By the fourth century, bishops were in contact with their fellow bishops in the collegial grouping known as the hierarchy (literally and significantly "rule by priests"). They grew more organized with the introduction of local meetings (conferences), then regional meetings (synods), and finally worldwide meetings (ecumenical councils). In turn, they would have their own "chairman of the board" or "super-bishop," the pope.

All this development was inevitable and needed as the church expanded dramatically and had to face many enemies. Still, there is no denying that, as a byproduct, a gap arose between clergy and laity, not to mention between bishops and priests, between the official hierarchy and the rest of the church. Even the word *clergy* is instructive. Originally it meant one's lot in life deriving from the custom of casting a lot to see what job one gets (much like our drawing straws). It was easy to transfer the notion of casting a lot to the one on whom the lot fell. He became "the allotted one"; hence, another easy move to understand "lot" or "clergy" as we do today. It was a natural word to be pulled into church language to refer to those whose lot it was to be bishop. From the bishop, it was a series of small steps to apply it to others surrounding him:

deacons, and priests, and finally all ecclesiastical officers of any kind that developed in the course of history. By the third century, clergy had really come to mean office holders in the church as over and against the regular Christians or laity.

This is not to say that in the early centuries there was not close cooperation on all levels. There was, and the greatest bishops in history were all pastors: Augustine, Ambrose, Basil, Gregory. We can easily sense the closeness in our earlier writers such as Clement of Rome, Ignatius, Justin, and Cyprian. It is in the later writings, such as the *Didascalia,* that here and there we pick up status signals. It probably could not be otherwise when clerical tasks became full-time occupations. Formerly teachers, prophets, and wandering apostles were part-time people still earning a living such as tent-making (Saint Paul). But now, with complexity, a full time commitment was needed. More and more of the part-time presbyters were drawn into full-time church care. More and more bishops, having absorbed the roles of prophets and teachers, were needed full time. As with everything else in life, it would be only natural that there would arise a certain distinction (and dignity) between the full-time and the part-time people, between the full-time givers and the full-time receivers (laity). Add to this the extraordinary privileges granted by the civil government such as exemption from taxes, civil service, and the ideal of clerical celibacy, then it becomes inevitable that a caste system would appear.

Even as far back as the third century, we read that Clement of Alexandria (d.c. 215) is saying that the bishop must take the first seat—as if Clement had never read Mark 9:35. The great Origen makes distinctions among the orders of bishops, presbyters, deacons, and laity. By the time of the Council of Nicea (325) the higher and more powerful bishops are quite distinct in rank from the lower and delegated presbyters.[1] Two hundred years later, Saint Benedict, the founder of monasticism in the West, would reflect in his famous Rule a fully established clerical caste system. In Chapter 62 he writes that any priests who seek to join the monastery should not be too quickly accepted. If a priest really perseveres in his desire —"if he persists strongly in this request" as Benedict put it—he may be accepted. Such a priest must know without any question, however, that the full discipline of the Holy Rule will not be relaxed because of his position. That is about as practical a commentary as we can get on the high estate that the priestly cleric had attained. As the trappings of the temple accrued to the bishops and priests and they became sacred personages, then they not only grew apart from the people but were positively enjoined to keep a certain distance from "defiling" secular occupations. Canon Law is full of such limitations. Furthermore, as the analogies grew between the levitical priests of the Old Law and the Christian priests of the New, so did the notion of levitical purity. The priests of old Israel abstained from sexual relations with their wives when they served in the temple. How much more the priests of the new Israel? And why abstain just then? Why not all the time? Why not celibacy as part and parcel of the priesthood? Gradually the notion grew. Soon some legislation was proposed, saying that priests could marry before ordination but not after. The Council of Nicea almost passed a law demanding celibacy.

Ultimately two traditions evolved. In the East, priests were permitted to marry before ordination but not after; and in the West, not at all. This was made official law at the Fourth Lateran Council in the thirteenth century. That it took so long in Christianity to become a Western law reflects something of the hesitation of that first Council of Nicea. For our part, we simply note that the law of clerical celibacy initially arose from the concept of ritual purity. Later, it would be re-enforced by the practices of monasticism.

It is little wonder that, with all of the precedents, the clergy did evolve into a caste system. It is little wonder that any laity who aspired to church ministry were ultimately made to fall within the bishop's orbit and become clericalized. The original lay ministries of subdeacon, exorcist, porter, and acolyte were thus clericalized and made stepping stones to the priesthood. Even when new religious orders were founded, it was felt quite necessary for its members, all laymen at first, to be ordained priests, even if they never did celebrate Mass. In due time, the unspoken law was that it was unthinkable that any official ministry could exist outside the clergy.

The most public and obvious demonstration of this clerical caste system was manifest at the liturgy. In spite of Paul's dictum that there is only mediator, the priest became precisely that. It was he who said Mass prayers, expressed the sacrificing intent, and stood literally between God and the people who watched the ritual silently. He became part of the near-passive magic in medieval times when just seeing the elevated host was enough to gain divine favor. Sacraments were sought as infallible watersheds of grace as long as the right ritual was used. The old Latin phrase *ex opere operato* ("automatically") reflected the popular notion of priest as power-bearer and conduit. Then, too, the introduction of the pure white host, laws concerning who could touch it, permission to clean the purificator, and the very architecture itself which distanced priest and people were all practical expressions of the new ritual purity and priestly mediatorship.

We can also sense another strand in the process of caste and clericalization. It has to do with priestly spirituality. And it began early. It is the spirit of monastic "other worldliness." The priest (ideally) barely tolerates this world. His real home is in heaven, for he deals with such august mysteries. His powers are those of Christ himself. How can he mingle with the rest of the people? Saint John Chrysostom sums it all up in his classic treatise on the priesthood. He writes, "For when you behold the Lord, immolated and lying on the altar and the priest standing over the sacrifice and praying and all the people purpled by that precious blood—do you imagine that you are still on earth among men and not rather rapt up to heaven?"[2] Here we see "holy apartness," a forerunner of emphasis in later centuries on priestly "detachment." Surely the priest is someone who is not of this realm. His powers to bring down Christ on the altar are awesome. Notice again that all the emphasis is on personal power, not on association with the community. The priest is truly sacred, celibate, defined by the altar. In a word, he is a monk, in the world but not a part of it. He was in fact truly other than worldly, beyond the reach of the ordinary laity who would never dream to attain to such holiness. And this ideal held firm for a long time in spite of the many ribald comments in the middle ages about ignorant and immoral clergy.

We have one final result in this clericalization process to describe. It is one most sensitive today: all of the ministries of the total church got swallowed up in the clerical state. As we page through our founding documents, we must remember how Ephesians 4:11-14 names the five ministries of apostle, prophet, evangelist, pastor, and teacher. We have noted already that 1 Corinthians 12 speaks of the diversity of roles, gifts, and charisms. But perhaps it is in Saint Luke's *Acts of the Apostles* (2:42, 44-47) that we get the clearest indication of the whole church at work. Luke describes for us there a closeknit community and how they continued in the teaching of the apostles, in praying, breaking bread, praising God, being in communion with one another, holding things in common, proclaiming the word of the Lord, and moving out to those in need.

In the more technical words of today, here was a group of people engaged in the priestly and prophetic work of Jesus. That is why Maria Harris is right in defining ministry simply as "the priestly and prophetic work of the church."[3] This means that the whole church is priestly insofar as it preserves tradition, celebrates ritual, and gathers community. The whole church is prophetic insofar as it speaks boldly the challenging word and serves the needs of others. These acts are not the property of individuals; they belong "to all who believed ... continuing daily with one accord in the temple, and breaking bread in their houses ... praising God ..." (Acts 2:42ff).

It is this understanding of ministry as mutual and belonging to the church that leads scripture scholar George MacRae to point out that

> Christian ministry is oriented to the needs of the Christian community and is rooted in the ministry of Christ. ... ministry gets its meaning from an understanding of the church, since the mission of Jesus is felt in the New Testament to be entrusted to the church, not to ministers, at least not as individuals.... [That's why Saint Paul, while he says that] God "entrusted to us the ministry of reconciliation" (2 Cor 5:19), nevertheless understands the church as a whole to be involved in his own apostolate. To the Philippians he can even speak of their "partnership in the gospel" (1:5). And indeed, the so-called "Great Commission" of Matthew (28:18-20), though clearly addressed to the "eleven disciples," must be heard, in the context of Matthew, as addressed to the whole church.[4]

Yet, with all of this background, with this clear understanding of ministry as belonging to a priestly and prophetic church, the bulk of Christians (the laity) were early reduced to a passive state in the life of the church. They retreated from active evangelization and witness, leaving such work to the professional monk and missionary. They adopted a second-class self-image and, most of all, they retreated from the liturgy of word and sacraments.

In fact, perhaps the easiest thumbnail test of just how far that retreat has gone would be to ask the average Catholic, "Who confers the sacraments?" The answer would probably be, "Why, the priest (or the bishop)." Until a few years ago, the answer would be the same if one asked "Who reads scripture at Mass? Who says Mass? Who leads the prayer?" But today the answers would vary. We suggest that a closer look at the sacraments would also provoke varied answers and give a more updated response. Before we look, we must state that there is a very real sense in which the priest "gives" the sacraments. As community presider, he does have official mandate in the public forum for the church's public sacramental actions. This is how it should be. We're not talking about that. We're talking about a style and a faulty theology that makes the sacraments clerical possessions to be dispensed, rather than community actions to be celebrated by all.[5] We're talking about the priesthood of all believers being totally subverted by the clerical priesthood.

It is well known that in an emergency any human being can baptize; even an unbeliever can do so. This points to the fact that there can be no intrinsic and inalienable "power" attached only to the priest to baptize. Again, it is surely his first right as public leader of the community, but it is also true that baptism is not so personally his that others can, not only share in it but, if need be, celebrate it. Confirmation, really an ancient part of Christian initiation, can be celebrated by the priest and not just the bishop. Most people know about such instances. What may be less known is that people have also historically been involved in the other sacraments.

As late as the sixteenth century, it was a solid opinion that a layperson could hear confession in an emergency. (Albert the Great, Saint Ignatius of Loyola, and even Thomas Aquinas called this "quasi-sacrament.") In fact, the whole system of private confessions arose with monks, who were laymen. Laypeople quite freely gave the anointing in the sacrament of the sick (extreme unction) for a long time. We have a letter from Pope Innocent I which says clearly that not only priests may use the oil prepared by the bishop, "but all Christians may use [it] for anointing when their needs or those of their family demand."[6]

As for holy orders, it is recorded history that for over a century, with papal permission, some abbots ordained their monks to the priesthood. Marriage, of course, is the mutual sacrament conferred by the contracting parties—although this too was brought into clerical domain by way of his necessary presence legitimizing the bond. Finally, there is the eucharist. Here we just have to recall the past pages: deacons, prophets, teachers, confessors—all presided at the eucharist at one time, or another. The point of all this is not that the priest has no rights in such sacramental matters. Obviously he does, and does so fully and officially as being ordained to the public forum and holy order of the church. The point is rather that the sacraments, as we know them today, seem so exclusively the priest's domain, not celebrations of the whole priestly-prophetic church. What we have come to think of as his personal power has given him sole and total power over the sacred, over the mission of Christ. We but stand and watch. Yet our brief, informative look at the sacraments in history reveals how far we have gone in giving over our priestly-prophetic gifts into one pair of hands; how far the mission of Jesus, entrusted to the whole church, has fallen to an individual minister.

That slow but steady process of surrender, begun in the sacraments, has been extended to all areas of the Christian life. In practice, this means that the impression has been created through the centuries that the church has, and can only have, one certified and credentialized ministry, the one bestowed by ordination. No matter how degreed or competent a lay minister may be, his or her standing is always emotionally and practically overshadowed and outvoted by any less able and competent clergyman. And this is so not merely because he is, in fact, ordained to the public forum and all community matters should come under his discernment—that is legitimate—but because the unspoken assumption is that his ministry subsumes all others. To this day, therefore, lay ministers, whether theologians, teachers, counsellors, whatever, still fail to gain a place in mutual ministry precisely as mutual, as priestly, and as prophetic. They still fail to gain the recognition that simple ordination gives to the priest. In fact, to go even further, all jurisdictional and administrative powers have come to be seen as extensions of his sacramental powers conferred by ordination. This is why decision making and administration are still in the hands of the ordained clergy rather than in the hands of all who collaborate in mutual ministry.

—2—

Before we move on in this section to examine the practical questions our history has raised for us in today's church, we must stop and backtrack a little. We must go back and pick up some of our themes and put them into the perspective of our own Catholic tradition so that we'll know where we stand. We'll say a few words about sacrifice and the eucharist, priestly images, and the priesthood of all believers.

Our survey has shown us that no cultic priesthood is to be found in the New Testament. Yet we wound up importing Old Testament levitical forms and imposing them on Christian ministry. How did this happen in the light of the Epistle to the Hebrews with its clear message of superseding the Old Law sacrifices? The answer is that this epistle was not universally accepted as a New Testament book and was controverted for a long time. The only thing most scholars seemed to agree on was that it was not written by Saint Paul. Therefore it got into the New Testament canon late and under a cloud. As a result, it had little corrective influence.

Still, the lack of influence of Hebrews does not account for the swift acceptance of sacrificial language in early Christianity. Yet even here such language, borrowed from the Old Testament, was radically adapted for the New. In the New Testament, worship is depicted as "spiritual worship" and spreading the gospel is called "priestly service" (Rom 15:16). So it went, using Old Testament words like "worship" and "priestly," but in new ways. Interestingly, however, the word "sacrifice" tended to keep its Old Testament connotations. It was used in a straightforward manner to explain the meaning of Jesus' death as previewed in the Last Supper. His death's meaning was placed in the context of the Passover meal celebrated at that supper. The evangelists themselves have Jesus speak of a covenant of his blood "which is poured out for many for the forgiveness of sins" (Mt 26:28). With this very real transfer of the sacrificial lamb of the Old Testament to Jesus as the Lamb who takes away the sin of the world in the New Testament, the groundwork is laid for dealing with the eucharist in such terms. So stable is this tradition that by the time of Cyprian (middle of third century) the eucharist is quite openly referred to as sacrificial and this becomes standard language by the fourth century.

Even with the notion of sacrifice attached to the eucharist so early, the concept became a source of controversy at the time of the Reformation. The Reformers had trouble, not so much with the notion of sacrifice as such, but with what appeared to be certain exaggerations and contradictions that had grown up around it. For example, the Reformers could not see how this eucharistic sacrifice could be repeated at every Mass since scripture proclaimed that Jesus' sacrifice was a "once and for all" affair. They therefore reacted to Pius V's catechism that talked about Christ as the victim "whose sacrifice is daily renewed in the eucharist." They resented the idea of a propitiatory sacrifice being offered through the human ministry of the priesthood because this implied that Jesus' sacrifice on the cross was not unique or sufficient. Today, however, once the Protestant Reformed theologians got past Catholic exaggerations, inflated ministers, and elaborate ritual, they themselves retapped the ancient tradition and were ready to admit that eucharist and sacrifice are compatible. One such modern theologian, speaking about his colleague, writes that he "is correct in saying that we are compelled to use sacrificial terminology about the Lord's Supper, because sacrifice remains a supremely important word to express our relationship to God, and because it is the divine revealed nature to give itself with a completeness of which Calvary is the measure."[7] About this same colleague he goes on to say, "Von Allen freely uses sacrificial language of the eucharist. It is the unanimous tradition of early Christianity, he holds, that there is an indissoluble link between the death of Christ and sacrifice...."[8]

Our point is that if there can be an agreement on relating the eucharist and sacrifice, then it is a rather natural step for Catholic Christianity to say that the one who presides at such a eucharistic sacrifice can properly be called a priest. Therefore while the notion of cultic priesthood does go beyond the New Testament, like so many other developments, it is not a distortion. On the contrary, as scripture scholar Raymond Brown says, the Catholic tradition has managed "to preserve, alongside the uniqueness of the sacrifice and priesthood of Christ, the Levitical consciousness of the sacred character of a special priestly service that brings one into contact with the cultic symbols of God's presence."[9]

Perhaps what has caused a problem for both Protestants and Catholics is that, while "priest" may indeed be a legitimate term to describe the one presiding at the sacrifice of the eucharist, it is woefully inadequate to describe the one presiding over the community. In other words, of all of the wide gifts and tasks of this community leader, there has been an undue focus on one single role. Of all of the proper titles, "priest" has stuck, to the detriment of the rest. If the priest is supposed to be reflective of Jesus, then it may be instructive to remember that in the oldest traditions going back to the New Testament, Jesus was given images other than priest to describe his mission and ministry.

In the earliest tradition, he was given the title of servant both as one who serves others (Lk 22:26) or, more significantly, as a suffering servant (Is 53) who gave his life as a ransom for many. Then he was given the title Son of Man (used almost 70 times in the New Testament) as a sign of his earthly ministry of service, and humiliation. Then he was called prophet, preaching the reign of God and calling forth the presence of God in people. He is called Lord in a confession of faith in his exaltation. And then, much later, he is called priest (Heb 8:1-2). Yet, among these almost half-dozen titles, it is this last one that has taken on cultic overtones and has become the almost exclusive content of the Christian priesthood. As one writer remarks:

> Development in the history of the Roman Catholic priesthood has tended to emphasize the cultic aspect to such an extent at times that this became the only, or at least the only significant aspect of its nature and practice ... if the ministerial priest is to be an imitator of Jesus Christ, there are many other aspects of ministry than this. And historical development could justify some other aspect being considered centrally significant.[10]

Theologian Walter Burghardt finds such "centrally significant" aspects in the course of history. He discovers five such distinct roles that have been emphasized in the Catholic priesthood.

They are: (1) the jurisdictional role emphasizing the priest as one who holds full authority from the bishop and gives authoritative teaching; (2) the cultic role, popular during medieval times, which saw the priest largely in terms of the performer of the sacred mysteries; (3) the pastoral role in which the priest is seen primarily as community leader and healer; (4) the prophetic role in which the priest is seen as the mighty proclaimer of God's word, the aspect chosen largely by the Protestant tradition; and (5) the monastic role in which the priest is viewed as the holy man, the guru, the spiritual director of souls.[11] So there has been a variety of meanings, a much wider concept of priesthood than the sole altar-oriented, cultic one. While this latter role is valuable, its one-sidedness has hidden a more holistic picture of the Catholic priesthood. As a Third World missionary writes,

> Concentration on the death of Christ—the priest reigning from the cross has colored the church's understanding of the ministry both of the church as a whole and of its ministries in particular. Both ecclesiology and the theology of priesthood have been based on the notion of Christ as priest. Ordination thus became a mystical configuration of the ordained to the priestly character of the Crucified and Risen One. It gave the ordained the power to represent sacramentally the sacrifice of Christ, and brought about a mystical and ontological change in the soul of the priest. There was a coherence in this theology of ordination. But when it was linked to the concept of the power of Christ ruling over the world, it inevitably led to a highly exalted, sacral-juristic conception of ecclesiastical office. There is no attempt here to attack the partial truth of this theology, only to say that it is not the whole truth; in a word, it is reductionistic, and obscures a more organic and complex whole.[12]

From a quotation such as this and from the comments of the past pages, we can see that in practice the word *priest* is far too narrow for today's ordained minister. Both in the Old Testament and in comparative religions, the word priest is so very specific and confined that the danger is that we might transfer it wholesale to our tradition. But, as we have seen, our concept of priest in Christianity encompasses so much more. It includes much of what we would call the prophetic ministry. It is very likely, of course, that we shall continue to use the term—we really don't have any other at hand that won't cause confusion—but we should mentally try to expand

and widen it as much as possible so that all the nuances of our history can be properly expressed and appreciated.

Meanwhile, as we stretch our minds about a particular priesthood of the ordained, we are forced to look at its other forms. In fact, the bible speaks of three expressions of priesthood. (1) There is the priesthood of Jesus described in Hebrews as unique and unsharable (10:14). Everything obviously must come under judgment and obedience to this priesthood—one of tears, compassion, suffering, and that total self-donation that earned for Jesus the title of high priest. (2) There is the priesthood of all believers, one shared alike by both clergy and laity and grounded in the communal act of baptism. The Protestant Reformers (remember: they were all Catholic Reformers) called our attention to this once more, even though it took us four hundred years to get moving on it. In this people-priesthood, we are reminded that we are all a "royal priesthood," a part of a priestly people, the recipients collectively of the mission and message of Jesus. (3) Our priesthood also consists in all of us doing "priestly service to the gospel of God" (Rom 15:16) and living sanctified lives in all that we do. This is no direct reference here to the eucharist, only to surrendered lives offered in service (*diakonia*) to others—which, after all, is precisely the Christ sacrifice we signal in the Mass. A whole people of God surrenders itself wholly to him.

If "surrender" is the key word of priestly sacrifice, then it is in this very real sense that, for example, Mary is a priest. She is the first Christian and shares with all Christians the priesthood of the faithful. She offered her own sanctified life in total donation, letting God's will be done in her according to his word. That is why she was praised by Jesus; not for her physical maternity, but for that sanctified life that "heard the word of God and kept it" (Lk 12:27).[13] Truly, Mary is the one who "offers and dedicates herself wholly to God, for him to use her freely at his choosing," and faith like hers "establishes us before God that we may stand in readiness to serve."

Those two quotations on Mary are remarkable not only because they are the words of the great Protestant Reformer, Calvin, but also because they hit the heart of the priesthood of all believers, as proclaimed by Vatican II, which said:

Christ the Lord, High Priest, taken from among men made a kingdom and priests to God his Father out of this new people. The baptised, by regeneration and the anointing of the Holy Spirit, are consecrated into a spiritual house and a holy priesthood, thus through all those works befitting Christian men they can offer spiritual sacrifices and proclaim the power of him who called them out of darkness into his marvelous light. Therefore all the disciples of Christ, persevering in prayer and praising God should present themselves as a living sacrifice holy and pleasing to God. Everywhere on earth they must bear witness to Christ and give answer to those who seek an account of that hope of eternal life which is in them.[14]

There is not, nor should there be, any opposition between such a priesthood of all believers and the ministerial priesthood. The former does not at all preclude the latter any more than Israel, as God's chosen people, precludes the emergence of the cultic priesthood. There is an intimate and necessary connection and difference between them.[15] As Hans Kung puts it:

All Christians have authority to preach the word, to witness to the faith in the church and in the world to "missionize." But only pastors with a special calling have the particular authority to speak words of reconciliation and absolution to the community in the meetings of the community, and hence to the individual believer. All Christians are empowered to share in the celebrations of baptism and the Lord's Supper. But only pastors with a special calling have the particular authority to administer baptism in the public assembly of the community and to be responsible for leading the celebration of the Lord's Supper in the community.[16]

Note how he roots the priestly presiding role in relationship to presiding over the community.

While we ponder these distinctions, we must be conscious

that while an ordained ministry of bishop, priest and deacon are necessary for the functioning of the church, it does not make the ordained minister any higher in God's sight than he already is by being a member of the priesthood of all believers through baptism. And yet, there will still be a Catholic people *proud that it continues to call its ministers "priests,"* because their role in the eucharist is distinctive through the example they give by the sacrifice of their lives, and because by their willingness to surrender themselves to God's will they offer a model of the general priesthood that all share.[17]

It is interesting to note, by the way, that the Protestant tradition has so heavily emphasized the general priesthood of all believers that particular lay ministries have been neglected. The theory was that all would be practical ministers. No special lay leadership was needed. No commissioning, installation, or recognition were called for. No religious orders of set-apart people were required. It hasn't worked out too well as these two Lutheran authors testify:

> From its refusal to call the ministry an order, Protestantism has usually concluded that there are not orders in the church. This conclusion is obviously hasty and has had disastrous results. Every human community or movement needs what we have lately called a "leadership cadre," a pool of persons whose circumstances are so arranged that they are available to serve the community's needs in a way that most members cannot be. Through most of the church's history, "orders"—of monks, nuns, widows, couples committed to mobility, and subsistence-economics, "deacons," etc.—have been the church's cadre, its pool of persons for shock-troop service in the mission and for service to the endlessly varying needs of the community. These orders have been distinct from the ordained ministry .... In Protestantism's pretense that it has no orders, its normal communal needs have driven it, in practice, to treat the ordained ministry as a general-purpose cadre ... it has distracted its ministers from the much needed special function that is in fact theirs. Sooner or later, the Reformation's functional understanding of ministry must compel us to rethink radically the whole question of leadership in the church.[18]

We end on a recurrent note in our reflections about our Catholic tradition. Often there is an unfavorable contrast made between charism and office, the implication being that the various charisms have been taken over and subverted by the institutional offices in the church. There has been a squelching of the charismatic gifts. There is much truth to this as we have seen (and shall see). Still we must put the theory into perspective beyond the hints given in the past pages.

Spontaneous charismatic ministries and established office are not necessarily opposed. Ministry and structure are not natural enemies. Both, after all, are the product of the same Spirit. True, when we look at the New Testament, we sense a narrowing down of Paul's church of charismatics but, as we saw, a new situation came into view. There was need for stability in the face of onslaught—doctrinal and physical. To meet the challenges, the church structured itself anew, through the office of bishop. There was nothing to oppose this, and in fact the scriptures quite support such a development. If Paul ascribes, as he does, all ministries to the activity of the Spirit, then it is hard to imagine that he would have characterized the development of office in the church as otherwise, as other than a gift of the same Spirit. Therefore it is good for us to recognize this as we examine in the following chapters the very real tensions that do exist between gift and office, ministry and structure.

CHAPTER FOUR

Yeast In The Leaven

—1—

In Morris West's novel, *The Clowns of God,* Carl Mendelius speaks to the Vatican's Cardinal Drexel about his friend, the lately resigned Pope Gregory, and asks about the encyclical that forced the pope's resignation. Asked if he read it, the Cardinal responds by saying,

> With great misgiving, obviously. I had not a doubt in the world that it must be suppressed. But I agree it contains nothing, absolutely nothing, that is contrary to traditional doctrine. There are interpretations that might be considered extreme, but they are certainly not heterodox. Even the question of an elective ministry, when ordination by a bishop is totally impossible, is a very open one—if rather delicate for Roman ears.[1]

That troublesome encyclical which is all about the imminent end of the world, does offer this "extreme" thought: that, at the end, since Christians will no longer be able to get together in large groups, "they must divide themselves into small communities .... When the priestly hierarchy can no longer function, they will elect to themselves ministers and teachers who will maintain the Word in its integrity, and continue to conduct the Eucharist ...."[2]

Obviously, the author of the novel did his homework and

read some of the ancient Fathers we referred to in previous chapters. The interesting point is that, ancient as these documents are with their "extreme interpretations," very few people know about them, even novelists, and until recently not many either cared or saw their relevance. But now their thoughts are more public and no longer considered extreme. Shocking, yes, but not extreme today. What happened to resurrect these notions?

Why didn't we know them before? What has caused these ideas to surface, ideas that we find so bewildering? To go further: Why, some might ask, don't we leave well enough alone and stop scandalizing the average Catholic still reeling from Vatican II's reforms? Things were so much more simple in the past—and secure. As one prominent laywoman wrote, "I confess that, originally, I didn't object to that hierarchial order; in fact, I thought it was a fine division of labor. There were all those people with special callings—vocations—to take care of things for me—to take care of worship, education, evangelization. I had only to attend, to receive, and to support."[3] But then she goes on to say, "It took a long time to grow into a realization that I am called to the priesthood of the people of God—that I, too, have calling *as a lay person.*" Between her first comment and her second comment, what happened? Or, to express it another way, can we uncover those factors which have moved us to take a second look at our church? The answer is in the affirmative and we shall look at five such factors, for they are instructive in reference to the whole question of ministry and church renewal.

The first factor to change our perceptions and focus we can classify under the general rubric of "research and discovery." We must be reminded often that in the past 150 years there has been an enormous outpouring of new discoveries about our past, both as a people and as a church. In 1880, for example, the now famous Rosetta Stone's hieroglyphics were deciphered. From that point on, just 100 years ago, the whole immense and highly cultured world of Egyptian civilization has been opened to us and with this a whole new context for reading of the bible. In the 1900's, Babylonia began to be uncovered. In 1971, a fragment of Homer's *Odyssey* was found that goes back to the third century of our era. A few years ago, archeologists think, they found the tomb of Philip of Macedon, the father of Alexander the Great. These are but a tiny portion of the discoveries that have been made in the last century and a half. All such discoveries, of course, have been made possible by the great leap in technology from echo chambers and aerial photography to carbon counting. The church and its book, the bible, have not been immune to such incredible discovery and research. For example, the *Didache* which we have several times used as a source, was discovered only in 1875, enriching our understanding of the first generations of Christians. The so-called *Epistle to Barnabas* was found in 1959, tucked away in the convent of Saint Catherine's on top of Mt. Sinai. A fantastic Gnostic library was discovered in 1945—that very influential heresy that heretofore we knew only from the remarks of its adversaries. Now we can read about gnosticism directly, understand Paul's epistles better, and await the continuing translations, and perhaps, revelations of further volumes.

In 1948, the famous Dead Sea scrolls were discovered by a shepherd boy in the caves near the Dead Sea. Found among the sect's documents was the earliest copy of the Old Testament we now possess. The community that produced these documents has shed much light on the first-century context of Jesus life and his followers. And so it goes. All of this research and discovery has had a powerful impact on the study of scripture and our understanding of the early church. Better tools, better research, better manuscripts and therefore better information—all have conspired to make us review our past and reset our present sights accordingly. Our cherished (and fairly recent) traditions have come under new judgment.

Just on this first point alone, it might be worth our while to pause and, in this context, to look again at the question of ministry. Recall that the old *Apostolic Tradition of Hippolytus of Rome* (likely third century) speaks so easily of bishops, presbyters, and deacons; it tells us that these were installed by the laying on of hands and adds that this was done explicitly in virtue of their liturgical roles. Then it goes on to say that other ministers, however, are simply installed (no hand-laying). It has in mind and mentions the widows, the readers, and the subdeacon. But then it goes on to say further that there are other ministries that are not validated by hand-laying or installation but by personal charismatic choice. These are the virgins who freely choose celibacy for the sake of the kingdom, the healers because they have been so gifted, the confessors, and the near martyrs. The point is that all of us are probably familiar with that first part, the part about bishops, presbyters, and deacons being "ordained." Now, in this fairly recently discovered document, we have a clearer picture of ministries *officially* recognized in other ways besides appointment —one by personal choice (the virgin), the other by the charism of the Spirit. What comes across is variety, sharing, and collaboration. This sort of research and discovery is bound to have its effect on our church in due time.

We have already traced, in the light of new documents, the absorption of the so-called lesser ministries into the offices of bishop and priest, and how ordination and not giftedness became the mark of authority. This historical process of centralization gives us the modern mandate to decentralize again toward a more shared ministry. Or take the clerical state. We have seen that anyone even remotely connected with the bishop and the liturgy was forced into the clerical state. Former lay ministries were made clerical ones. Ordinary Christians were lectors and acolytes, exorcists and porters before they were pulled into the clerical state. Yet we know, for example, that Origen, antiquity's greatest theologian until Augustine, both read and expounded the scripture at Caesarea while still a layman. It was commonplace for laypeople to take communion home with them so that they might receive during the week. It was usual for them to take a full and intimate part in the preparation of the catechumens. All this is a way of saying that the records show that the early Christians saw themselves indeed as a "royal priesthood, a chosen race," and holiness resided in them collectively. Research and discovery has helped us to follow the path of separation of such holiness from the people of God (or, in Paul's more primitive phrase, family of God) to its transference to the altar, and from the altar to the priest; or if we would express it another way, from primal and fundamental call to ministry grounded in baptism to that bestowed in ordination. Knowing this has been the cause of our faltering recovery of a more shared and collaborative ministry in the church.

Research and discovery have had their effect even officially, the result of which has been that in 1972 Pope Paul VI declared that those so-called minor orders were to be changed. The lector and acolyte, he said, would be rerouted as canonical ministries and no longer be called *orders* at all, but simply *ministries*. Exorcist and porter were to be dropped. This was a right step. Unfortunately, in the following year, most likely as a result of a bureaucratic lack of communication, a decree came out from one of the Vatican congregations instituting "Extraordinary Ministers of Communion." It was hard to figure why something that is a right by baptism and the ordinary practice of the early church needed to be designated as "extraordinary" and required episcopal mandate, especially only a year after a sensible effort to declericalize the ministries.

—2—

If research and discovery have been one factor in our current self-consciousness as a church and in our changed perceptions of priesthood and ministry, the shortage of ordained priests has been another, second factor. Certainly the critical shortage of priests has made the implications of the previous chapters sharper and more urgent. The clerical ranks have been depleted and continue to be so by resignation and death on the one side and little replacement on the other. Many Christian communities throughout the world, but especially Latin America and Africa, are without priests. Around 1975 there were some 130,000 parishes throughout the world, some 44,000 without priests. Missionary posts reveal that while 4,100 had priests, some 79,000 did not. It is estimated that in Latin America there is one priest to every 1,065 Catholics and in Europe the situation is not much better.

In the United States in the years between 1966 and 1978, there were 10,000 fewer priests and a decline of some 25,000 seminarians. Meanwhile, the average age of the clergy, like the country at large, is getting higher and higher. There is not only the "graying of America," but the "graying of the clergy" as well. In 1981, the major Archdiocese of Newark, New Jersey rejoiced over one of its largest ordination classes in years and the largest in all of the United States for that year: 19. The Archdiocese of Chicago came in second with 16. As much as anything, such pitifully small numbers for such large areas shows the plight of a diminishing number of clerics.

Nor is the future promising. According to a recent study, the priest population is expected to decline for the next 20 years. It is estimated that by the year 2000, the diocesan priest population will be about 17,000, which is approximately what it was back in 1925 when the Catholic population was only one-third of what it is now. All of this, of course, puts a special and necessary emphasis on lay ministry and, as such, has been a potent factor in the reshaping of the modern church.

The third factor giving rise to our current change and development is the rise of the worldwide charismatic movements—including Cursillo, Marriage Encounter, and Charismatic Renewal. These are fundamentally movements *for* and *by* the laity. They are essentially democratic, open to men and women. Their proliferation is a testimony to the endurance of that democratic Spirit, first preached by Peter on the first Pentecost. Perhaps the current explosion is a kind of Freudian reaction to a too long suppression or absorption of giftedness by the institution. Basically, such movements need no institution, they need no clergy. The Spirit breathes freely.

Maybe it's a reaction to all institutions in general and the sense of powerlessness among the people that global institutions engender, or maybe it's a prophetic retreat from the false salvation so abundantly promised by advanced technology that has given the world both insecticides and pollution, energy and toxic waste. Salvation is better sought in the old ways of myth and giftedness. Prophecy and healing are back in vogue, but so is the demonic. How else to explain worldwide hunger in the midst of plenty and the madness of stockpiling overkill weapons? If prophecy, healing, and the demonic were a part of Jesus's world, they are a part of ours too, and they need Jesus's basic response. It is this sort of reaction that is tilting the current church off its hierarchial axis toward more community-based, ministry-oriented communities whose ultimate dignity and source is not ordination but baptism. The charismatic movements are symptoms rather than causes of world unrest and ecclesiastical impotency. Some would claim these symptoms are creative.

A fourth factor, a cause of ferment in our church, comes

from Vatican II which became in its own way a kind of prism of change, for this council did not so much invent new changes as reflect them. We might take note here of three fundamental notions from this council that would greatly validate a shift from sole hierarchial control to a collaborative clergy-lay type of ministry. The first is seeing the church as a mystery rather than as an institution, thereby opening the way for many gifts. The second is insisting on the priesthood of all the people of God, which obviously is going to have impact. The third is sensing the church as a inheritor of a genuine mission rather than as a haven for the saved, thereby reminding all of their common innate evangelism.

The words of the council have rung loud and clear: "The lay apostolate is a participation in the saving mission of the church itself. Through their baptism and confirmation, all are commissioned to that apostolate by the Lord himself." And, "These faithful are by baptism made one body with Christ and are established among the people of God." Since the time of the council in 1963-65, the language has become stronger as is evidenced in a document issued by the United States bishops on the fifteenth anniversary of the Decree of the Laity. Even its title tells it all: "The Laity: Called and Gifted." It says things like this:

> One of the chief characteristics of all men and women today is their growing sense of being adult members of the church ... laymen and women feel themselves called to exercise the same mature independence and particular self-direction which characterize them in other areas of life .... The adult character of the People of God flows from baptism and confirmation which are the foundation of the Christian life and ministry .... Baptism and confirmation empower all believers to share in some form of ministry. ...Because lay women and men do experience intimacy, support, acceptance and availability in family life, they seek the same in their Christian communities ... This is leading to a review of parish size, organization, priorities, and identity. It has already led to intentional communities, basic Christian communities, and some revitalized parish communities ....[4]

In such words we should not underestimate the episcopal insistence on mutual baptism as the source of *all* ministries any more than we should underestimate Vatican II's decision, in its document on the church, *Lumen Gentium,* to place Chapter 2, "The

People of God," before the chapters on clerical ministry in the church. The significance is the deliberate and revolutionary shifting of the concept of church away from a hierarchically structured one to an organically structured one. In a word, the radical primary focus is placed on community, and off hierarchy, as the essence of the church.

It follows, therefore, that it really does not make any difference what function or authority or responsibility or charism a person exercises within this general community (not that they are all equally important or vital); they all exist one way or the other for the building up of the body of Christ, as Paul reminds us. We are ministers, says Vatican II, because through our common baptism we belong to Christ. Ordination is seen as one kind of ministry (although admittedly special and sacramentalized) among other baptism-based ministries within the church. To be a priest is not to be all ministers in miniature. Ordination confers a particular ministry, not all ministries. All the people of God share in the one basic priesthood grounded in the common life of Christ. All ministries and all spiritualities, whether lay or clerical, are aspects of that, and this common source rules out any caste system.

It is interesting to observe, by the way, how these concepts are so prophetically reflective of our national mood and our consciousness, namely, that we have enjoyed the efficiency of high technology but not necessarily the joy of living. They reflect a desperate need of a country such as ours that has discovered that the much commercialized "be number one, self-fulfillment" agenda has only produced loneliness and depression. As one insightful pollster writes, "Our advanced industrial society, for all its strengths, has long harbored a fundamental weakness: it has prodigiously generated goods and services, but it has been seriously deficient in creating some of the basic conditions of human community."[5] And then he adds a perceptive note whose application to ministry and today's church is evident.

> Not all workers are engaged in the search for self-fulfillment, but those who are retaliate for the lack of incentives by holding back their commitment, if not their labor. They resent sharp class distinctions between employees and employers. They do not automatically accept the authority of the boss. They want to participate in decisions that affect their work. They prefer variety to routine, infor-

mality to formality. They want their work to be interesting as well as pay well.[6]

With proper adjustments, we can go back and read this quotation inserting those words that tell us of the church authority and lay ministries.

Some further words significant for the church:

There are scraps and shreds of evidence that American culture is evolving toward a new ethic of commitment. The word "commitment" shifts the axis away from the self (either *self*-denial or *self*-fulfillment) toward connectedness with the world. In the interviews conducted, people express a longing for connectedness, commitment and creative expression—a poignant yearning to elevate the sacred and the expressive side of life and diminish the impersonal, instrumental side ... the hunger for deeper personal relationships shows up in our research findings.... By the beginning of the 1980's, the number of Americans deeply involved in the Search for Community had increased from 32 percent to 47 percent, a large and significant jump in a few short years.[7]

All this demonstrates that there is a new mood abroad and that the creativity and agitation of emerging lay ministries is not merely an aberration of our church but national movement of the people. And all this, of course, puts pressure on the institutional church. The traditional church ministries of bishop, priest, and deacon who absorbed all ministries in their own persons are now being asked to share them.

—3—

The fifth and final factor we must look at may, although recent, prove to be the most powerful force of all in changing the face of the church. It is the emergence of what is called *Basic Christian Communities* (BCC). A Basic Christian Community, the product of the South American church chiefly, is a group of Christians bonded by intimacy, frequent contact, and mutual aid. They are deliberately and fundamentally grounded in religion, and, as one might expect from the continent of liberation theology, a religion that is not passive or self-serving but one with an eye to political and social betterment. As one member of the White Fathers' community observes of a Base Community in Africa, "In our parish we like to say that to be a good Christian one must follow three—not two—rules: love God, love your neighbor, and build a better world. We expect basic communities, therefore, to become actively involved in development work. We encourage them to participate in their village government and to work in whatever way possible for the betterment of the village."[8]

The Base Communities are quite serious about the process of building up of lay leaders and the lay ministries. The leader, significantly, is not considered in any authoritarian way but as a "first among equals," whose claim to leadership is precisely his or her claim to service. Furthermore, such leaders carefully walk the line between their technical training and their own personal charismatic gifts. There is always the concern that they are not distanced from the people. In many places, there is great cost to the leader. That same White Father observes:

> The animators of these communities are simple men and women, farmers with large families for the most part. The one additional thing they have in common is a deep and unshakable faith. Most of them came to this faith as young men and women, but once having found Christ and chosen him deliberately, they have followed him in spite of seemingly insurmountable obstacles. One young man told me of how his relations—believers in traditional religion—after trying repeatedly and unsuccessfully to get him to undergo the usual fertility rites, had finally resorted to anointing him with flour as he slept.

> Most of the community animators live in the midst of hundreds of non-Christians. They represent one very small spark of Christian faith in the average village. Most of them receive a visit from a priest or sister only five or six times a year. They usually manage, not without difficulty, to come to the main parish or to some other central location for training seminars two or three times a year. Aside from those rare contacts, their faith is nourished almost completely on the spot. Nevertheless, they survive and even thrive.[9]

The Basic Christian Communities began in Brazil precisely because there was a severe shortage of priests. Yet, they felt the need for unity, identity, and nourishment. So they rerouted their parishes into a federation of small communities and from this came the Basic Christian Community. Today there are some 50,000 of them in Brazil alone. The formation of such communities begins with people gathering to read the gospel and reflect upon it. From these reflections comes the deep conviction that they *are* the church, and this consciousness is encouraged by the institutional church. Next comes a reassessment of the roles of ministry, both lay and clerical, and a distinct reshuffling of ecclesiastical priorities. Gottfried Deelen outlines the noticeable differences between the conventional parish and the Basic Christian Communities this way:[10]

Point of Comparison	The Parish	The BCC
Structure	hierarchial	democratic
Doctrine	very important with emphasis on tradition	not the main thing: emphasis on the gospel
Run by	clerics	laypeople
Emphasis on	religious practice	moral values
Social Origin	middle class and upper layers of society	lower ranks of society
Universality	the church of Christendom	the "one door" church
Sacraments	instruments of salvation	signs of salvation
Religious values	for the individual life	for common action
Center of the Church	Rome	the poor

As we study the comparison, we cannot help catch a tone very reminiscent of the first Christian communities we read about in the New Testament. Anyway, the Basic Christian Community becomes in reality an ecclesiastical grouping tied to popular culture, intolerant of paternalism, either of church or state, and one which has concluded that "a clerical church, where in practice the priest alone personified the church, should give way to the church of the people in which the lay person could participate to a higher degree. What should be sought after was not so much a church of the masses, but a church made up of groups that practiced reflection."[11]

Prayer and teaching, therefore, are important in the Basic Christian Community, and this harkens us back to the roles of prophet and teachers. The doctors of theology or the priests do not necessarily do the preaching, but the simple people, anyone who can lift up consciousness for a liberation derived from the gospel and who can make people aware of the intimate connection between faith and life. Leaders, in this light, be they preachers, catechists, or pastoral planners, are seen as peer pilgrims who both nourish and travel along with the people of the Basic Christian Communities as they journey.

It is quite extraordinary that, for the most part, the official church in South America has gone along with this type of community, as did Pope Paul VI. They realize that the times call for new structures even to the point of declericalization. They know that the people have a need and a right to exercise ministry, make their own statements, find their own voices, and that the health of the church does not depend exclusively on the authority of the bishop or the priest. The bishops are even prepared to face the question, we shall see ourselves later on: will those natural community leaders, arising from the people, be free some day to preside at the eucharist?

Meanwhile, for our purpose, it is enough to know the existence of these Basic Christian Communities, that they are spreading through the rapidly growing Hispanic churches in the United States and will have a most profound impact on the whole question of ministry and shared responsibility, particularly as we ourselves are exposed more and more to pastorless parishes. We do not want to canonize the Basic Christian Communities for they are not perfect and carry the danger of elitism. But they are symptomatic of what's happening in the church. They have a direct relationship, for example, to a publication in a country far north of them. The eminent journal from Canada, *National Bulletin on Liturgy,* dedicated an entire issue to the topic: "Sunday Liturgy:

When Lay People Preside" (May-June, 1981), and had this little introduction:

> There is a growing number of communities in Canada and in other
> countries where no priest is able to come to lead the Sunday celebra-
> tion of the eucharist.
>
> In many places, pastors are selecting and training men and women to
> lead the people of God in Sunday worship. Sent by their bishop,
> these leaders call together the believing community, and invite them
> to praise God on the Lord's day.
>
> This issue of the Bulletin offers models of celebrations for those who
> lead these Sunday celebrations.[12]

Meanwhile, as we think all this over, we must recognize
quite openly the obvious issues that are connected with these
critical approaches. We must be prepared to face the questions that
the existence of Basic Christian Communities and the other four
factors we have examined pose for us. More to the point, we must
be ready for considerable tension in the church of the twenty-first
century, for there are powerful ramifications here that will not go
away. Some of these we will expose (but not necessarily give solutions to) in the next chapter.

CHAPTER FIVE

Tensions In The Assembly

—1—

We will inevitably experience severe tensions arising from the factors we saw in the last chapter. Here we are in our time of history when new insights and old traditions are interacting to change radically what we consider our unaltering Catholic heritage. We hardly seem to be over the changes already unleashed by Vatican II and suddenly, here at our doorsteps, are more tensions, more problems to be solved. Or are they opportunities? Whatever they are, we must face them squarely for, in the long run, they are all variations on the critical theme of ministry: how it is to be rerouted, shared, reshaped, and what effect will this have on our current structures of church order. In a summary fashion, we will look at six areas: ordination, the election of bishops, celibacy, women in the church, priestly identity, and authority.

First of all, as the various lay ministries multiply and as the influences and experiences of the Basic Christian Communities grow, there is bound to be a rise in tension and frustration between gift and ordination. For instance, many of the laity are deeply involved in various facets of church work and are totally dedicated to evangelization and prayer. Yet, they have to stop at a given point and let a priest, who may only be a visitor, come in to do the "priestly" work. For example, if some layperson, along with his or her entire community, has taken someone through instruction and spiritual journeying leading to baptism, why should he or she step aside to let some uninvolved priest baptize? And why should this be true especially if there are no priests available and the layperson knows that at one time in the early church the laity baptized? The same is true for the dedicated layperson who is gifted to care for the sick but who cannot give the sacrament of the sick even in the long term absence of the priest, even though the laity at one time in history did so. (Not even a deacon could give this sacrament.)

People are asking, "Why did that man have to die without receiving the sacraments when I was right there at his bedside?" It's not a question here of authority, for indeed authority must be respected. (A sympathetic mayor cannot grant a reprieve to the prisoner about to be executed, but only, let us say, the unsympathetic governor; it belongs to his office and authority alone.) It may rather be a question of a more widely shared ministry in those things that at one time did belong to the laity.

The tension we are seeing here is grounded not only in plentiful laity *versus* few priests, but also in charismatic tradition of the past *versus* present legislation; the gifted of the community *versus* the impositions of the institution. It is largely legislation, we recall, that determined who does what sacramentally and spiritually. In the early church, remember, virgins, widows, and teachers were not inferior offices, and they did ministry. Confessors were allowed to preside at the eucharist, although neither ordained nor consecrated. the people of God, in theory and tradition, have gifts and direct access to God. Saint Paul reminds us that "it is God who establishes us with you in christ, and has commissioned us; he has put his seal upon us and given us his Spirit in our hearts as a guarantee" (2 Cor 1:21, 22); and he tells his Roman audience that "you yourselves are full of goodness, filled with all knowledge and able to instruct one another" (Rom 15:14). This is not to deny the role of the priest or his rightful role as community leader. It is rather to focus, as of old, on the needs of the community, and to ask who shall minister in cases of urgency. It is to ask about broadening the recognition of the ministerial gifts of the people.

The Basic Christian Communities, for example, where there are no ordained priests, are creating a push from the bottom up to give wider meaning to ordination, and at the same time are subtly begging ordination for their naturally gifted leaders. They are implicitly challenging the standard Western seminary training system where men are taught in a European-American medieval scholastic intellectual tradition and not from grass roots experience, such as they know in the Third and Fourth Worlds. It is the Basic Christian Communities and others that are posing the question that, in the absence of duly certified ordained priests, why cannot they enjoy the same privileges and freedoms of the first century? Why cannot they use their native talent, shape their own theology, have their own prophets, teachers, plurality—and the ordination of their leaders who are not necessarily trained by Aquinas or Calvin?

If they are asking this (and they are), the next question cannot be far behind: where there are local congregations without a priest, cannot they be permitted to raise up their own? There is ambiguity and contradiction here.

> The anomaly resulting from the fact that the Christian church recognizes the right of laypeople to baptize but refuses them the right to celebrate the eucharist seems to have been perceived.... The even more surprising anomaly of granting the laity the right to engage in catechesis or to perform the liturgy of the word (a privilege of the bishop), while denying the same laity the right to preside at the eucharist under any circumstances, is felt in every place where *ordained* celebrants are lacking.[1]

We are not talking about local communities taking this on themselves to do—although some have—for "there is an ancient and modern awareness that no Christian community can call itself autonomously the ultimate source of its own ministers."[2] We are talking about the official church restoring the wider ministerial traditions of the past. As Cyrille Vogel puts it:

> It is rather odd that the first liturgical function which the laity were historically recognized as having, in exceptional cases, namely the right to baptize, should still be acknowledged today by all the Christian churches as belonging to all laypersons (even if not baptized) whereas the right to offer the eucharist is refused to these same laypeople. Moreover, these laypeople obtain without difficulty the right to teach, although this is a basic episcopal prerogative, it would seem that from a theological viewpoint, the right to baptize and the right to teach should raise as many problems as does giving believers the right to offer the eucharist.[3]

The issue of such rights is particularly acute when it comes, as it so often does these priestless days, to emergency situations. Could not the church recognize the celebration of the eucharist by an unordained Christian if no priest were available? After all, we saw that this is how the presbyter-priest got started. The bishop alone was considered in due time the only legitimate presider of the eucharist (Brown). Yet when this became quite impractical, as numbers and geography increased, the bishop delegated this function to the presbyter-priest. Some would argue that since we are in a similar situation today, the same process could be followed. Once more, natural or chosen lay leaders could be delegated to preside at the eucharist at least on an *ad hoc* basis.

To the question of such laypeople presiding at the eucharist in an emergency, more and more theologians are giving an affirmative answer. Such would include Kung, Schillebeeckx, Kasper, Breuning, Lehman, and Rahner among Catholics, and Fries and Pannenberg among the Reformed theologians. It is also interesting to note that the Catholic-Lutheran dialogue in this country on "Eucharist and Ministry" concludes, that in view of the silence in the New Testament, it is difficult to say what is really necessary for the eucharistic ministry. These opinions also seem to underscore the question that there is therefore no inherent "power" in the priest concerning the eucharist but rather, as we have suggested, any such "power" resides in the community and therefore, by extension, in the one who presides over the community.[4]

None of this is meant either to promote illegitimate ministries or challenge the legitimacy of church office or hierarchial authority. The church has a right to choose its eucharistic ministers and set up "quality" controls. Nor is this a challenge to the priestly ministry as such, for installation here is a sacramental act, while others are not so considered, and so we do have a different level of importance. Rather, we are talking about a style and a vision that allow a wider sharing of ministry, especially in emergency situations. We are thinking about the genuine possibilities of recognizing or delegating native leaders—at least on an *ad hoc* basis—to preside at the eucharist within their own cultural context, not in a Roman-based, Western context alone.

Edward Schillebeeckx catches the possibilities nicely:

There is no direct link between contemporary office of the church (the episcopate, the presbyterate, and the diaconate) and an act of institution on the part of Jesus himself while he was on earth. It is clear from historical analysis that already existing models in the Jewish and Hellenistic world and concrete demands made by the historical situation of the church influenced the factual structure of the leadership of the community. Even seen from the sociological point of view, a social group such as the church would be unthinkable without official ministries. The sociological process within the church which caused the episcopate, the presbyterate and the diaconate to emerge from an originally greater number of offices in the church (many of which disappeared later or merged with others) is, however, correctly interpreted on ecclesiological grounds (the church is, after all, the "temple of the Holy Spirit"), as the work of the Holy Spirit, the Spirit of the exalted Christ. Even though these offices do not go back to a historical act of foundation by Jesus, they are, by virtue of the pneumatic nature of the apostolically ordered Church, themselves the fruit of the Spirit and not simply the result of a sociological process of growth. In this sense it can be said that these church offices are based on a *jus divinum* [divine law]. Such a "divine dispensation" can, however, be so understood that it includes and at the same time makes possible a historical growth of various forms and divisions. As long as the church is able to distinguish the sign of the Holy Spirit in it, restructuration is therefore possible, not only in the past (this is quite clear from history), but also in the future.... It is therefore possible to divide and regulate all the powers of those who are now called bishops, priests and deacons differently as long as this is done in a way that really enables the church to function as the church that was founded on the apostles and prophets with Christ as the cornerstone.[5]

—2—

The election of bishops may seem a foreign element in our discussion of shared ministry, but not when we see it in the wider context of community, which so far has been the basis of the direction we are taking. In fact, it is quite critical for us to take a look at the question here, for tensions in the assembly can come from this source. Many may not know that until 1917 election was quite the common way that bishops were chosen. After 1917, Canon Law (canon 329) introduced a real innovation by declaring that "the Bishop of Rome freely appoints them." This canon says, furthermore, that if anybody, such as a king or emperor and parliament, still has the privilege of election due to old historical concessions, then this remains strictly by way of concession, not by right. It has only been, then, some 65 years that the technical right of the pope to appoint bishops has been in vogue. This does represent a departure from the nearly 2000-year tradition of election, even though this was many times more honored in the breach.

This election tradition goes back early. The *Didache* speaks of it. The *Apostolic Tradition of Hippolytus* clearly says, "let him be ordained as bishop who has been chosen by all the people ... by the consent of all, let the bishop lay their hands upon him." Even the rather authoritarian Saint Cyprian considers this to be of divine right. Pope Saint Celestine writes in the fifth century, "Let a bishop not be imposed upon the people whom they do not want." His successor, Pope Saint Leo writes, "He who has to preside over all must be elected by all.... Let a person not be ordained against the wish of the Christians and whom they have not explicitly asked for." Thus the tradition of election. Actually, it was gradually eroded by the political pressures of history, pressures from the secular rulers who wanted to control the episcopacy and resistance offered from Rome by restricting the election of bishops to the clergy. Later, in the sixteenth century, it let the Catholic monarchs appoint bishops. It was only in the twentieth century that Rome finally won the uncontested privilege for itself.

The interesting thing is that a man was ordained to the episcopacy in his own locale. They would not think of bringing in a stranger from the outside, as we do today. The community called its own people, even against their will at times. Some of the greatest bishops had to be forced to accept the honor: Martin of Tours, Gregory the Great, Ambrose, Augustine. The reason that the local church chose its own bishops was practical in more ways than one. The people were in a position to check a man's faith and so, in this very real sense, the people themselves bore witness to the apostolic faith. It was understood, moreover, that from the very first moment of election that this was the work of the Holy Spirit, and so the election was not so much a process of democracy as it was a manifestation of the Spirit's work. So there was no strict hierar-

chial understanding of ministry, as though it was handed down
from on high. Rather, it was the combination of both: the Spirit
working through the people and the leadership validating the
choice. In this way also, the bishopric remained fundamentally a
ministry of the church.

The point of all this can be seen in the light of the past
pages. It provides a challenge to a too heavy emphasis on the consecration of the bishop—and that of the priest—at the expense of
the communities needs and consent and familiarity. The election of
bishops is bound to be caught up in the same questioning as the
choice of local leaders and priest. The desire of the community to
know its leaders, to have its cultures honored, and to have those
over them who can be with them and of them and speak their
language must touch the whole papal process of appointees. As
shared ministry multiplies, there will be further pressure to break
up enormous dioceses that keep the bishop a remote figure and
bind him too heavily into administration. Many of the world's
2,300 dioceses are much too large. In no way do they permit a sense
of community and the development of ministry. It has been suggested by responsible observers that some 25,000 to 50,000 more
dioceses be created.[6] Only in this way can proper evangelization of
the large cities take place. Only in this way can grass roots communities reclaim their identity with a proper leader. For many, this
is crucial, for they are convinced that the grass roots communities
are the one genuine place where renewal of the whole church can
take place. As Jurgen Moltmann says, "My thesis is a simple one:
The local congregation is the future of the church. The renewal of
the church finally depends upon what happens at the grass roots
level. And renewal at this level awaits, it seems to me, the conscious
reclaiming of the gifts of the Spirit on the part of the laity."[7] One
of the essential lay gifts to be reclaimed is to have a voice in those
who are their leaders. To this extent, the foreign appointment of
bishops and the needs of the native community is another tension
to be resolved.

—3—

Celibacy connected with the priesthood is quite another
thing from celibacy connected with being a Christian. The ideal of

celibacy for every type of Christian is to be found in the gospels themselves. It was Jesus himself who made the point that some people, finding the real treasure and pearl of the kingdom, could not do otherwise than to leave all things, including marriage, for its sake (see Lk 14:26; Mk 10:21). There *are* eunuchs for the sake of the kingdom of God. But, as Jesus remarks, not everyone can or must accept this, but only those whose inner logic of deep religious conversion demands it. Paul concurs (1 Cor 7:7, 8; 28-35). For such a charism to move from a religious option for the average Christian to a necessary condition for the priesthood has been a big step. We have noted that this step was taken under the influence of the Old Testament levitical priesthood. The priest should refrain from sexual relations with his wife during his service at the temple. This was extended to the Christial priesthood and for all the time. Celibacy's tenuous connection with the priest, then, is one of ritual purity. Such a connection was resisted in the early church. We saw how the Council of Nicea refused to endorse it as mandatory, how the eastern part of the church did not demand it, and how it took until the thirteenth century to become a law in the West. It is, then, a discipline, not an inner condition.

Celibacy is extolled as an "emptiness for God" (Aquinas) and Henri Nouwen writes that

> Celibates live out the holy emptiness in their lives by not marrying ... by not filling their lives with events, people or creations for which they will be remembered. They hope that by their empty lives God will be recognized as the source of all human thoughts and actions. Especially by not marrying and by abstaining from the most intimate expression of human love, the celibate becomes a living sign of the limits of interpersonal relationships and the centrality of the inner sanctum that no human being may violate.[8]

This is true for celibacy in general and still not a necessity for priesthood, although Archbishop Joseph Bernardin, in a lovely meditation on the ministerial priesthood, insists that there is a connection. He says that the church presents celibacy as something more than a discipline. He calls it a "qualification" that enhances one's witness and ministry. He quotes the 1971 Synod of Bishops which tells the candidate for the priesthood that he "must understand this form of life not as something imposed from without, but rather as an expression of his own free giving, which in turn is accepted and ratified by the church in the person of the bishop." The Archbishop calls celibacy a "personal charism which is inherent in their call to the priesthood as it is mediated and affirmed by the church."[9]

The point is, however, that if a candidate for the priesthood does not make celibacy an expression of his own "free giving," he is not accepted for the priesthood. The point is that if celibacy is a charism "inherent" in the call to ministerial priesthood, then Saint Peter was excluded as well as all those bishops who, as Saint Paul said, "must be above reproach, the husband of one wife" (1 Tm 3:2) and the entire litany of those who form the continuous Eastern tradition. This kind of history and argumentation does not in any way invalidate a most beautiful charism and one that, in its faithful expression, has been one of the glories of the priesthood and the church. But such history and argumentation will continue to provide the material for pressure for a married clergy in the face of the current shortage. Tension will continue to mount as, for example, former Roman Catholic priests who have gotten married organize the first international synod in Rome in 1983 on, significantly, the feast of Peter and Paul, the one married, the other celibate—both pillars of the church. An estimated 50,000 priests have left the ministry to get married and some, not all, would like to function officially again. A union of married Catholic priests was founded in Italy in 1975. These people on the one side who have left the clerical state, and communities on the other side who are seeking their own leadership, will combine to create the increasing tension and call for a married clergy.

Furthermore, in this context, we should not forget our current crisis of many local parish communities which are without priests, a crisis forcing more and more of them to rely on the leadership of unordained men and women. With each passing decade, the possibility increases that future generations of Catholics could emerge without those sacramental and especially eucharistic celebrations that have characteristically been at the heart of Catholic identity. The dilemma is that if the church continues to insist on celibacy as a condition for ordination, it may run the risk of losing the eucharistic focus of future Catholic communities because of the lack of priests to lead them. It's a dilemma that will increasingly force church leadership to make a choice:

either to defend no options to celibacy whatever, thereby eventually defining Catholic communities by something other than the traditionally central eucharist, or to ordain married men.

The place of women in church ministry usually raises the twin questions of ordination to the priesthood and equality of acceptance. We need not review here all of the arguments for or against the ordination of women. It will continue to be debated for a long time. It may be pertinent, however, simply to present two quotations. One is from that scripture study commissioned by the bishops on the priesthood in 1971. There is a footnote in the study that says,

> By way of an aside, it might be noted that Paul actually says nothing in 1 Corinthians 14 that can be construed as an argument against the ordination of women to the priesthood and their consequent participation in the authority of the church. His dicta are disciplinary, clearly conditioned by the cultural taboos current in Judaism and Hellenism and of a strictly local and temporary nature. [10]

The other quotation, from 1979, is from the executive board of the Catholic Biblical Association. It says that an examination of the biblical evidence shows

> that there is positive evidence in the New Testament that ministries were shared by various groups and that women did in fact exercise roles and functions later associated with priestly ministry based on the praxis of Jesus and the apostles, disciplinary regulations and the created order cannot be sustained. The conclusion we draw, then, is that the New Testament evidence, while not decisive by itself, points toward the admission of women to priestly ministry. [11]

We let these quotations stand as we remark that many women are not interested in ordination. They are far more interested in equality, especially in the equality of being recognized in any of their pastoral ministries. More and more, they resent being put down, especially if they are qualified in their fields. A recent study from the Center for Applied Research in the Apostolate (CARA) in Washington, D.C. and the Gallup Poll both indicate that women's service in the church is inadequately used. The study drew this portrait of the typical woman in ministry: she is middle-aged, well educated, married, the mother of a small family, has some college education but little training in her specific ministry, and looks upon her involvement as an important part of her life. About 75 percent of women's ministerial activity falls into the categories of education, liturgy, and administrative support services. In these areas, functions traditionally assigned to females continue to dominate: teaching, secretarial work, fund raising, and so on. The study also showed the hispanic and working-class women are conspicuously absent from ministerial roles. Beyond this study, other resentments surface, especially from women who work closely with priests. Women resent decisions being made in their absence, low prestige categorizing, the use of sexist language, the fear from less educated and less talented priests, second-class status in the church, and any aura of patronization.[12] This whole area of man-woman, priest-female pastoral minister is fraught with terrible tensions. Perhaps, from the priest's point of view, what is at the bottom of it all is the enormous threat to his already endangered self-identity. Many women in ministry identify this as the basic problem.

That identity is much in question today. After all, Vatican II and other documents we have seen have put such stress on baptism rather than ordination as the basis of ministry. This has cast a shadow of doubt about the priest's ministry. Is this job being subverted by all those "others"? At one time, the salvational treasury was in his hands exclusively. If one wanted to be saved, one went to the priest. He was the one who dispensed blessing, forgiveness, sacraments, and mediation. His presence or absence at the death bed made the difference between bliss and damnation. Because, as we saw, his was a personal power, it didn't matter whether he was holy or scandalous, capable or inept. His was "the power and the honor and the glory forever." And today?

Today, people tend to view God's presence as pervasive in ordinary every-day life. The theologians put this perspective in the language that speaks of grace as coextensive with creation. If God's presence is so free, so to speak, and if salvation is so universally available and not just found in the sacraments and or the priest who gives them, what use is the priest? How important is his role? The question is further aggravated by the increasing sanctuary duties taken over by the laity, from reading the word of God to taking communion to the sick. If there is a priestly identity crisis, we can see why.

We have rightly noted in Chapter Three that the priesthood as we know it today is not necessarily a distortion of the New Testament witness. The priesthood was a natural paradigm to explain Jesus and his work in the people we call priests. We saw that the priest indeed has preserved "the Levitical consciousness of the sacred character of a special priestly service that brings one into contact with the cultic symbols of God's presence" (Brown). But, we also took note of heavy baggage that has accrued to that role. There is some uneasiness as that top-heaviness gets dismantled. We are forced into the position of asking, as the process goes along, about the priest's identity, about his role today.

The first thing that we can say about the priest's identity is that he embodies the values of the group. Someone must be the symbol of what the community values and the gospel it stands for. Someone must be in the public leadership position who is entrusted with the community's symbols. Two authors, a Methodist and Anglican, catch this aspect well.

> Liturgically speaking, the purpose of the ordination rite is for the designation of symbol-bearers or leaders for the church. The ordained ministry is merely a function of the church, necessary only because of the church's need to have someone bear and illumine its symbols of identity so that it may be about its God-given business. In ordination the community bestows its blessing upon the ordained, recognizes God's call of this person to the priesthood or pastoral ministry, and prays for God's gifts to enable this person to fulfill the designated function of priest.

> It is not that other people could not pray, preach, teach, heal and administer sacraments as well or better than the priest. It is that, when the priest does these things, he or she functions as the symbol-bearer for the community, under orders from the community, as the officially recognized, corporately designated person to bear and interpret the community's shared symbols. And that makes all the difference.... No one can be a priest by private desire to be one. The community expects the person to be able to testify to a personal vocation from God to the priesthood, but the community also reserves the right to confirm or reject the call. The call is from God *and* God's church.[13]

The priest, then, is the community symbol-bearer.

From this aspect of his role flows another. He is the "sacrament of Christ the Head in the formation of community" (Dodd). That is to say, he is the focal sign of community always-in-the-making. He is the sign, if you will, of Jesus gathering, of rallying the community around the Christian symbols. He leads in the shaping of the great sacrament, the church, which is the sign of Christ. In this leadership capacity, he is thereby entrusted with the "highest level of sacramental intensity of the Word" (Rahner). That is, while the whole assembly is entrusted with the living word, the priest is entrusted with its highest expression which reaches its fullest meaning in preaching within the eucharistic liturgy.

William McElvaney, a Methodist pastor, says that ordained ministers are called

> to many *functions* but to only one *focus*. Our single focus is the Word, Jesus Christ. We have too many functions to be classified as specialists in the classical or usual sense, yet in the covenant of the ordained we are specialists of the Word. In many roles and through diverse functions, we have just this one purpose of lifting up and living out the word. We are representatives of the Transcendent Incarnational Lord. The ordained ministry of leading and empowering the people of God in and through God's Word in Jesus Christ is a task of proclamation, administering the sacraments, and representing the whole church *for which no one else in either church or society is trained*. To be sure the total ministry of the Word is a mutual ministry of the whole people of God visibly proclaimed in baptism and validated in the act of confirmation. An adequate theology of ministry can recognize the ordained as a specialist of the Word, and at the same time one who encourages a shared, collaborative style of leadership in and through the Word.[14]

We should note something remarkable here, namely, that all of these profound and genuine identities of the priest revolve precisely around the pristine notion of community. The priest rallies the community and keeps it true to itself. He presides over the "church gathered" as the laity carry the gospel to the "church scattered." He is the leader who keeps the vision going. He preserves the body of Christ from forgetting who it is just as a vital laity preserves the Body from forever looking backward. He preserves the body from amnesia while the laity saves it from nostalgia (Frankl). To this extent, the priest *is* a community man, an institutional man, even though that phrase rubs us the wrong way in our anti-institutional days. He does represent an institution.

> No matter how charismatic, how prophetic, even if called to protest the sins and corruption of institutions, of the church itself, the priest must represent more than his personal insights.... [He] cannot stand outside of [the] institution.... This institution is the setting where faith is born, and grows; this institution is the locus and focus of worship; this institution is the community of love. This is what the priest represents.[15]

He belongs to the public forum.

Because the priest is the preserver of the community's symbols, community gatherer, one entrusted with the highest level of the word, then it is precisely such presiding over the community that entitles him to preside at the eucharist. And furthermore, as community leader, presider, and preserver, his role takes on a functional emphasis as well as a symbolic one. He must enable or empower the people to achieve their goals and tasks and he must keep the faith-reflection of the community ongoing. And so, the priest's role does have a definition. His ordination is to community leadership. As Avery Dulles writes,

> Ordination is a recognition of the gift of leadership, and at the same time a sacramental commissioning that empowers them to govern the community in the name of Christ. Jesus acts through the ordained and commissioned ministers, even beyond their power to understand (see Jn 11:51). By their obedience to pastors, within the sphere of their proper competence, Christians are privileged to submit to the Lord himself, in accordance with the formula, "He who hears you hears me" (Lk 10:16).[16]

All of the foregoing points up the obvious truism that holy order is literally a sacrament directed to the *order* of the church so that, as Vatican II expresses it, "all according to their proper roles may cooperate in this common undertaking with one heart." The church celebrates the sacraments as an expression of its intimate life, but such celebrations require "that everything is ordered to the benefit of the whole church and to its upbuilding (1 Cor 14:5). Through the exercise of this sacramental ministry of holy order, the whole sacramental reality of the church is expressed...."[17]

In summary, then, the priest is "ordained" to *holy* order: to establish an orderly and proper celebration by the community of the mysteries of salvation. Within its long and varied tradition of priesthood in the Christian church, the priest does indeed have an abiding and critical role, an enduring gift to offer.

The priest's gift may be enduring, but is his role? This is the kind of sensitive question that is being raised with a new urgency today. In other words, can the priest resign his presidency and still be an honorable man? Currently any priest who leaves the ministry is considered less than full of integrity, a traitor really, or one with ulterior motives. Like the old Charles Healy cartoon in *The Critic* in which the priest is saying, "I am leaving the priesthood because I believe that the parochial school system is obsolete. Because I am distressed by the church's failure to meet the social needs of the poor. Because the American bishops are not implementing the decrees of the Vatican Council. Because of the irrelevance of the church's message for the modern world. Because I have doubts about the literal sense of the scriptures." And then in the last drawing the priest adds, "And my fiancee is leaving the church for the same reasons." True, there has been a lot of rationalization and subconscious motivations for leaving the priestly ministry. But this does not in fact cancel the many genuine and sensible reasons why a man might do so. The key question is, Why can't he do it with honor and dignity?

David Ashbeck gives some sensible thoughts here. He uses the analogy of an admiral who resigns his office. He says:

> By resigning from a particular office within the community called America, he does not resign from the American community. He may have resigned for a number of reasons: he wants to enter some other occupation, job, or whatever; he has grown tired and worn out from his military office; he may no longer find the office fulfilling. Whatever reason, the man resigns; he is still considered an honored man within America; he is not labeled a 'traitor'; he also continues to live his American life faithfully.[18]

So, too, for a variety of reasons, the ordained minister may wish to resign. Perhaps, also, to take up an active ministry again someday. What prevents him from doing so? Why is he not accorded the same legitimacy and honor as any teacher who switches jobs or a Supreme Court judge who resigns and goes into private practice? If popes have resigned their papal ministry (for example, Pope Celestine, a canonized saint) why not pastoral ministers?

The popular mind doesn't see it that way. The average Catholic tends to make an exact parallel between ordination and marriage: both are forever. But, of course, there is no exact parallel. Marriage is a God-given natural bond whose terms are fidelity and permanence. Ordination is a church ceremony whose terms are dictated by the church. To be chosen as a presider over the community and its eucharist does not carry the same divine mandate as marriage. Or else the popular mind sees the priest as one who receives a permanent "character" on his soul at ordination (often confused with an "indelible mark") and this mark or seal or character makes him "a priest forever according to the order of Melchizedek." True, holy orders, baptism, and confirmation do "characterize" one in a permanent relationship to the Lord and his community. But this has nothing to do with switching positions within the Christian community anymore than it does with a cantor becoming a lector. A priest should be able to switch jobs as much as any other baptized person within the same ecclesial community. He maintains his once-and-for-all abiding relationship with the community but it is exercised in another way or not at all. As Ashbeck says, "Treating a competent, ecclesially faithful, resigned priest with disdain, barring him from regular, non-ordained ministries within the church ... is prejudicial and discriminatory...."[19]

The final tension in the assembly is the large issue of governance. In today's climate, as we mentioned at the beginning of this book, priority is given to baptism, charism, collegiality, and competency when it comes to questions of ministry—lay or clerical. The problem comes, of course, in the conflict between such an ideal and the real of an old system. In this system authority had clear and well defined lines: it was given by ordination regardless of charism, competency, or collegiality. And it was given as unquestioned. There is much less tolerance of this today. Not that people do not appreciate authority; it's the manner, absoluteness, and exclusiveness that draw fire. This is especially so as more and more laypeople move into positions of pastoral ministry and in fuller roles in liturgical and sacramental leadership. While lay ministries proliferate, access to governance in the church still remains at a standstill. If the laity are told that they share in the mission of the church through baptism and commitment, then why should they not have some responsibility for decision making in the church? Yet the door to decision remains closed.

That the hierarchy intends to keep it closed for the time being is evidenced by the fact that it will permit local lay ministries to exist and even regional ones, but not global ones. Some have suggested that the ordination of the married deacons may be one breach in the walls of governance and they may build a bridge between the lay community and the hierarchial office. This remains to be seen for the 5000 or more deacons in the United States who are running their own gamut from total fulfillment to total neglect and have their own versions of the identity crisis.

Perhaps the authority issues surface most acutely on the everyday practical level where full time and certified lay ministers have no voice in decisions, and no job stability. A new bishop or pastor can hire and fire the full time lay minister at will, unlike the cleric. For the most part, laypeople have no avenues by which they might challenge, arbitrate, or take advantage of any due process system, although some steps are being taken here.[20] These are serious tensions that future years will increasingly bring to a head.

Anyway, such are six areas of tensions, grounded deeply in the theory and the theology of the church and it is only a thoroughgoing mutual understanding of the church that will help resolve them. Meanwhile, let us end on an upbeat note, a word from Archbishop William F. Borders of Baltimore, who said to his priests:

> I think the fires of renewal have purged us of our exclusive claim on ministry. But the magnificent gold that has come from the burning is the enormous outpouring of gifted men and women whose ministries we have not even been able to catalog yet, whose impact on the total Christian community is just being felt. If we have lost our exclusiveness as ministers, we have taken over a new role—that of minister to other ministers, enablers of those who are called to serve one another.[21]

Chapter Six

Not So Gentle Confrontations

—1—

Massachusetts Congressman Tip O'Neill likes to tell a story about a man named "Honest Jake Bloom." Honest Jake was well known in the Boston area because of the help he gave three generations of immigrant families. He owned a little variety store and he would extend credit to the poor immigrants, helping them get started in their new land. As Honest Jake neared his sixtieth birthday, a group of people whom he had helped decided not only to give him a party but also a large gift of money. Jake received the money gratefully and began to use it on his own revitalization. He had his teeth capped, dyed what hair he had, and bought a hairpiece. He went to the health spa and trimmed down. He traded in his old horned-rimmed glasses for contact lenses. He bought a stunning new wardrobe. Then he boarded a plane and a few hours later, the new Honest Jake Bloom hit the beach at Miami. He met a beautiful young woman, asked her for a date, and she accepted. But before they could go out on the date, a thunderstorm came up. Honest Jake was struck by a lightning bolt and he died instantly. In heaven he said to God, "After all those years of hard work! I was just trying to enjoy myself a little. Why? Why me?" And God said to him, "Oh, is that you, Jake? I'm sorry, I didn't recognize you."

After all that heavy stuff in the last chapter, we need a little comic relief. But the joke has its point for us Catholics too. Would God recognize the changed church? Those six areas of tension we just looked at so briefly—who would have thought a decade or two ago that they would even be items for discussion? The "bad news" is that there is more. We have a few more problem areas to tackle. But "the good news" is that there are only a few of them and, unlike the previous ones, they do not necessarily deal with the heavy theological implications. They deal more with the everyday, nitty gritty annoyances and irritations that people feel as new and old ministries clash a little. Our investigation is something like seeing the movie *Nine to Five* where a few observant office girls take on the traditional chauvinistic male office boss. But not to look at the "office" tensions here is not to see a church painfully on the move; worse, it is not to deal with what we must.

The first issue is one of language. This may not seem much, but words and titles are terribly important and not to have words is not to have a significant means to deal with reality. But, the simple fact is that, at this point in our development, we don't have terms to describe fully the meaning of ministry. We do know that we have the ordained priest and we have the bishop and the deacon. Then we have the unordained laity. This leaves us neatly with the categories of clergy and laity but does not account for the growing and shaded areas in between.

Look at the variety. We have those engaged in ministries who are untrained volunteers. Then we have trained volunteers. We have part time paid people in ministry and full time paid people in ministry, most of whom are professionally trained and degreed. Some lay ministers are in secular work such as running their own professional workshops hired out to the church or in the publishing business viewing it as an apostolate. Others are in "churchy" work such as DREs, pastoral associates, and what have you. What is the distinction among all these ministers and between them and the ordained? Not the theological distinctions but the sociological and institutional distinctions? Should the word *minister* even be used? Some have urged the restriction of the term only to those part-time or full-time people who have been publicly recognized by the local church community, or the church at large (such as DREs and eucharistic ministers). These would be the people who have been recognized, commissioned, installed or appointed.

Others have an objection to all this installing and commissioning business. They ask, Why make so special what in fact was ordinary ministering in the early church? If we go on installing and commissioning all over the place, we're going to wind up, sooner or later, with a clericalized laity. As we pointed out before, why must one be specially mandated by the bishop to distribute communion and yet, at the same time, in virtue of baptism, engage in the equally critical public reading of the word of God in the assembly or teaching the apostolic heritage (catechism) without any special mandating? True, human nature demands some public notation; but then, why not use the word "recognition" rather than installation and commissioning? The latter imply a delegation from on high while the former implies an acknowledgment by the community peers of one's giftedness.

Theologian David Power phrases the question for many when he asks,

Why is it necessary to commission laypersons and even to set up special canonical offices for services which are normally theirs in virtue of their membership in the Christian community? Some discipline and control may be necessary, but hardly a canonical office or a commissioning and appointment in such official form. There are only two broad genders of liturgical ministry: that which is attached to baptism and that which is attached to order. To serve at table, to give communion to others, to bring communion to the sick, to read the scriptures, to instruct in doctrine, to make the word known to non-Christians, are not tasks which require a commissioning over and above baptism and the gifts of the Spirit.[1]

Anyway, back to our question: What do we do to all the new ministers? What do we call them? We can see it more clearly if we put it in outline. All of the baptized fall into the following groupings:

ordained
non-ordained
part time
full time
volunteers
paid
unrecognized
recognized, commissioned, installed

A new group, more or less permanent, committed to public service of the church as a vocation, not a career, have taken on formation (spiritual and professional), competency, accountability, and are filling a need recognized as important by the local or universal church.

There are kinds of combinations to this outline. Notice that neither male nor female religious are mentioned. Some would insist (Archbishop Weakland) that the religious life, in spite of words to the contrary, is not fundamentally a ministry in the church at all. Rather the religious life is a distinct and powerful living out of the evangelical counsels. A Mother Teresa and her sisters, for example, would not be considered as primarily "doing ministry," but living the gospel imperatives of poverty, chastity, and obedience, which overflows, as from a source, into good works. Their rationale is the gospel community that spills over into ministry, not ministry that accidentally has people living in community.

Sticking with the outline, there is a question mark before the last group that describes a new breed of ministers. These are neither the part timers nor volunteers but those who are in between. These are the people with a real calling to full time work in the church as a vocation, a more or less permanent vocation at that. They are not ordained but that seems to be the only distinction. These are the people entering co-educational seminaries and formation groups and studies for full time church work with no intention and no desire to be ordained. But they have no identity, no work to describe themselves. Of late, some have coined a very apt phrase, "ecclesial ministers," and for the time being this seems to be a good term.

On the other hand, we should also know that others are quite content to have ambiguity as far as naming the various new ministers. They would prefer the fuzziness because it still gives room for flexibility to a whole area which is new and which has not yet settled down. They fear that a too-soon naming will confine development. Finally, there is a side issue too, which we acknowledged before. The danger is that volunteers might withdraw as more and more trained ecclesial ministers take over. The implication once again is that Western-trained, intellectual and degreed people really do represent the best in the church. Their increase both in numbers and professionalism might replace the natural gifts of the people, perhaps even patronize the people and limit representation to certain ethnic and economic groups.

Meanwhile, while we're waiting for clarifications about the term *ministry* some steps have recently been taken by the administrative committee of the National Council of Catholic bishops (NCCB) and the U.S. Catholic Conference (USCC). These bodies voted to restrict this term in all of their future official documents to mean either the ordained ministry of bishop, priest, and deacon or what they call the "designated lay ministry." This latter refers to the work of those people officially designated to act as acolytes and lectors or in any other such canonical offices that might be established in the future by the Holy See. The term is also allowed to be used of functions established by a bishop and carried out by commissioned laypeople. All other jobs and functions shall hereafter be referred to simply as "Christian service."

This, the committees said, is "the response to the call to serve that flows from the sacraments of initiation ... [and] requires no formal action on the part of ecclesiastical authorities." The committees added that for such "designated lay ministries" there must be formation in doctrine and spirituality. As we indicated above, not everyone really wants such lines drawn right now. There was, for example, an immediate reaction from another bishops' committee, the Committee on Doctrine, which pointed out that "while consistency in NCCB-USCC use of 'ministry' has value, it is premature to attempt a precise definition of the word. A rush to judgment would only disrupt discussion of the serious theological problems which definition raises." Again, we observe the problem of language to describe a new phenomenon in the Catholic Church.

—2—

If suitable terminology is yet to be discovered, so are the proper relationships between the ordained and the non-ordained. (Even here the language problem is apparent: we define the lay minister in the negative, yet a priest would not like to be called a non-layman.) The priest (or bishop) has all of the canonical power while in canon law the layperson has none. Yet they are expected to work together in a shared ministry. In conflict, the clergyman will remain and is assured of his job either in his present position or elsewhere. This is because he belongs to the institution and the institution is committed to take care of him. Laypersons can sign contracts to do church work, of course, but the contracts are not for very long and have natural termination dates. In fact, the very existence of contracts for the layperson only serves to underscore the fact that the priests are not required to sign contracts. They are always employed just by being priests. These factors make any clergy-lay relationship fundamentally unequal. It's like working in the same office with the boss's son.

Another sensitive point in trying to come to some workable relationship between clerical and lay ministries is the question of accountability. For most professional laypeople, accountability is part and parcel of their daily lives. They are theoretically and most often practically held to accountability for their performance, their dress, behavior, professional development, continuing education, current skills, and all the rest. Very few, if any, clerics have ever had to participate in a professional job evaluation. Some may argue that the priestly ministry is beyond such mundane evaluation, for this call is on a different level. But this only fogs the issue, for "ecclesial" ministers feel the same way about their calling. The burden of stability and accountability all seems to be on one side in the clergy-lay ministerial relationship.

Perhaps the whole area is just too new. Both lay and cleric still have a great deal of recent history that they bring to the relationship. The old mythologies of the untouchable priest and the world-tainted layperson are still strong. Brother Loughlan Sofield has identified three such hang-ups or fears on either side of the relationship.[2]

The first fear for the laity as they approach church ministry is that of being "eaten up alive." That is, they don't mind helping out here and there, but they have no intention of making church work a career. It's the old cliche of going to the rectory for a Mass card and coming out full time CCD coordinator! That's not quite what they expected. Furthermore, the lay-person who does get into church ministry of any kind often finds less and less time allowed for the family so that he or she becomes a stranger at home. Frustration and burnout are also possible: no relief, no time away from the job, no restoration of spiritual resources. No wonder this first fear is right on target.

Another fear is what is called the "holiness paralysis." This is the traditional lay lament that I am not worthy, not just to have the Lord enter under my roof, but for me to enter under the Lord's roof, such as rectory or convent. It's a kind of Uriah Heep posture that so sinful and spiteful a person as a layman or woman could teach religion or distribute holy communion. If only the people knew that I was small-minded, filled with anger and lustful thoughts. If only they knew that I harbor secret doubts about my faith and that I don't "buy into" all that the Catholic Church teaches. The distance between the taken-for-granted holiness of the priest and sister and themselves is more than some laypeople can bear. This colors their relationship both to ministry and to the clerical co-minister as well. The final fear of the laity is the lack of confidence—"'I'm only a layperson" sort of thing—and surely this must affect the clerical relationship.

On the other side of the hyphen, the clergy have their threefold fear as well. The first is the ingrained and programmed burden of "false expectations." These include not only the false expectations the clergy have of themselves but also the ones that the laity have of them. Most men were trained in the old seminary mold whose monastic spirituality programmed them to be "all things to all men." Therefore, although only one or two percent of the general population, they feel constrained by some interpretation of the gospel to do everything for the 98 or 99 percent. Often the people themselves reinforce this. "I want Father to bring communion to my mother." "Let's ask Father." Or witness the criss-cross communion lines to receive the host from consecrated, not profane, hands. All of this is an unreal and heavy burden that has caused so much authoritarianism and, in other directions, so much alcoholism and burnout. Still, the priest is haunted by these false expectations and brings these compulsions to bear on his relationship with the laity. His identity and his supportive strokes, he feels, depend on this. The people expect it.

The second clerical fear flows from the first. Priests generally are out of touch with their feelings and their own basic needs.

There is a need to be in control, to be liked or loved, to feel important, to feel safe and secure, and to feel good about oneself. The system does not permit much admission of these needs (they seem somehow so "unworthy") and does not permit many avenues for expressing one's feelings. The result is that frustrated or unexamined needs and truncated feelings will have a strong effect on relationships with the laity, usually in the form of falling back on authority.

Finally, there is the plain truth that most priests lack the simple skills in dealing with people and groups. The (old) seminary curriculum trained the priest to perform. As a result, he has considerable skills in performing liturgy, the sacraments, and various blessings. But he was not trained to minister or promote the ministries of others; his skills do not lie in working with groups, listening and letting things happen. He brings this outmoded posture to new ministerial situations and this is bound to cause friction. So, add it all up: you take the priest's inherited hierarchial authoritarian stance, add to it the fears generated by training, mix that with an unsure laity burdened with fears of burnout, unworthiness, and lack of confidence, and you have a whole basketful of practical relational conflicts that must be worked on and overcome if there is to be any kind of genuine collaboration and shared ministry. We should be honest enough to dig a bit further now and recognize that, in many instances, beneath these various fears, often lies the very real issue of power.

—3—

If we mention power, we must mention power's most public form in North America: money. Money is not so much the issue when we are talking about volunteers as it is in speaking of those ecclesical full time, vocational ministers in the church. The least that such people need is a written or verbal agreement that their jobs are guaranteed for a sensible period of time. Their stay should not be subject to the whims of the new pastor or parish council. Adequate salaries must, in justice, be considered. Normal advancement opportunities must be honored. Job descriptions must be clear and the worth of each person's ability must be honored. These musts and shoulds sound like elementary justice and they are, but frequently the priest or religious is unjustly preferred on the unwritten and unproven assumption that they know more and are more competent, and they are financially cheaper to have.[3] The absence of elementary courtesy and justice in these matters is a form of power abuse as well as indifference to the charism of each person. A lack of cooperation here makes the ideal of shared ministry nigh impossible.

Another area in the clergy—lay relationship that has nettled some people is quite an authentic one and goes deeper than most. It was an area raised by a group of laypeople at a Chicago meeting. They objected that all the talk they heard from the bishops about ministry strongly implied that genuine lay ministry meant ministry connected with sanctuary. Lay ministry, the bishops seemed to be saying, is concerned with the liturgy and teaching. The laypeople pointed out that, while these areas are legitimate for those in part time or full time capacities, the vast majority of the laity are in the world. It's the world that is their proper sphere of witnessing to the gospel. Such laity should not be made to feel somewhat less "ministerial" by devoting most of their time to the "secular."

Once again, there is unexpressed fear that a clericalism among the laity will occur with the "church" lay ministers becoming a caste apart, whose task it is to minister to the poor, and the "worldly." But those not involved directly in the sanctuary ministries ought not to feel inferior to those who are, for it is the world that is the church's mission. It is in the neighborhood get-together, the ethical decisions of the marketplace, the funny and hurtful tensions of family life, the public issues, from better schools to nuclear disarmament, that demand the church's perspective in the presence of dedicated laypeople. The stuff of daily existence calls for daily gospel incarnations and so the church has to be involved in the world. As one lay minister put it:

> We are called by God to speak his Word within the church, our rehearsal stage for speaking his Word in the world.... The laity, by their very vocation, seek the kingdom of God by engaging in temporal affairs and by ordering them according to the plan of God. They live in the world, that is, in each and all the secular professions and occupations.... I see lay ministry as a complementary ministry. I

see the lay minister, particularly the professional minister, as the primary symbol and leader for the layperson in discerning his own apostolate beyond his immediate environment, to the needs of the world that are crying for him or her.[4]

This last quotation leads us to a theologically practical problem concerning ministry: the problem of the particular, of parochialism, of in-growth. If we want to get down to the very roots, ministry is grounded in the basic needs of all human beings. The simple fact is that we are all born with needs and therefore depend on others to fulfill them. Sometimes this is looked upon as a regretful, embarrassing, and sad human deficiency. On the contrary, to have needs is a positive thing. Having needs is full of value for it is fundamental to our humanity to know that we are finite, that we are never self-fulfilled but are fulfilled in and with others. The glory of humanity is fulfillment in God. It's a restatement of Augustine's observation that our hearts were made for God and are quite restless until they rest in him.

The truth is, then, that no human being just exists; rather, we exist in relationship from the moment of our birth. Our needs are a necessary correlative to human completion. And ministry is our code word for reacting to those needs with a sense, that we, in the very act of ministering, are God's instruments. The question we are raising here, however, is that we must always be alert to the truism that ministry is always larger than we think, always more universal that we would have it. Of course, we have to minister to the group we know. Of course, people have to carve up their ministerial turf for right order. Of course, we must serve the particular as we know it. Yet, somehow, we must keep the universal vision in mind. That is, the partisan thrust of good ministry must eventually give direction to a world mission. If it does not do that, if, to be practical, local parish ministries promote only the welfare of the group and do not lead the group to something beyond itself (the whole basis for social justice), then a closed corporation syndrome sets in. The way is open to petty rivalry, jealousy, infighting, or, worst of all, self-satisfaction. All this comes down to the gospel fact that the universal mission is the necessary imperative of particular ministry.

A final word. Throughout this chapter, we have been talking about accountability, governance, stability, power, job evaluation, money, advancement—all terms borrowed from the worlds of psychology, sociology, and business. That such terms are so readily used these days in the church is a tribute to the impact that the social sciences have had. Nor should we be surprised at this since the church is a human community as well as the body of Christ, an institution as well as a mystery. But we should take note of the tension involved.

Here is one side of the tension: Without evaluation, accountability, and the like, it is easy for the ordained or nonordained minister to slip into individualism and idiosyncracy. Lack of any measurement can lead to self-doubt as well. it is often troublesome for the clergy, for instance, not to have some indication of "how they're doing"—a favorite question—not to have a sense of competency. For a long time, some people have thought it odd that all kinds of measurements, passing grades, tests, and graduations were demanded before ordination and none whatever afterward. It was a hard educational and competence battle to get into the priesthood or the ecclesial ministry and no battle at all to stay there. To this extent, ministry of all kinds, including the priesthood and episcopacy, ought not to escape what the rest of the world (theoretically) demands: "give an account of your stewardship." Give the community some handle on its ministers, some way of ongoing testing, some means of verifying and discerning competency, some way of legitimately terminating the obstructionist.

But there is the other side of the tension: The gospel is basically so upside down to all human business measurements. What standard or competency tests deal with the folly of the cross or that philosophy that says that to die is to gain and to lose one's life is to find it? What organizational model fits the servanthood-leader model? How do we evaluate love? How do we escape the flatminded measurements of production, promotion, and product that turn us into a giant corporation? How does prophecy survive the relentless testing of political and social norms? What tools do the national standard measurement corporations and testing centers have for a failed and crucified Messiah? Are eminently sensible questions the only ones to ask?

To see both sides of the tensions is not to cancel the point or deny the needs. It is to place the necessary secular measurements under the judgment of the gospel. Of course, we need some standard, some evaluation. Of course, too many ministers, clerical and lay, are untouchable, unmanageable, unconcerned, and uncontrolled. Of course, accountability is a genuine form of community justice. Still, a mighty discernment is also needed lest we strike down the teacher and so modify the behavior of the prophet that we mute the voice we desperately need to hear.

Enough of these tensions and cautions. It's time to close with a brief reflection. In the movie *Little Big Man,* old Lodgeskins had a favorite remark. He would say, "It's a good day to die." And his final prayer was, "I thank you for making me a human being. I thank you for my defeats. I thank you for my sight. And I thank you for my blindness which has helped me to see even further." Our somewhat monotonous cataloging of ministerial frictions has been like this prayer in this sense: we are all aware now that we are joint "warriors" in the army of Christ, a pacifist kind of "onward Christian soldiers." We are forever bonded through baptism and ordination to the newly common unity of what we call ministry. Things have been, and likely will be for a good time to come, terribly untidy. Still, we have to thank God for the genuine victories so far and for the defeats so far. We have to thank God for seeing our traditions and guessing at our future. Yes, we thank God even for the darkness of tension and friction and mutual groping, for in such dependent blindness, we hope the Spirit will help us all to see even further.

CHAPTER SEVEN

Building Blocks

—1—

An expensively dressed woman was sitting alone at a table in an elegant New York City tearoom. A prosperous looking man stopped at her table and said, "Pardon me, Madam, but I could not help noticing that enormous diamond ring you are wearing. It is magnificent." Obviously pleased, the woman replied, "Thank you very much, my dear man. It's the Heppleworth diamond, you know." The man looked puzzled. "I'm sorry," he said, "but I don't believe I have ever heard of the Heppleworth diamond." "Well," she said, "it's just as large and clear and beautiful as the Hope diamond. Also, like the Hope diamond, the Heppleworth diamond comes with a curse." To which the man replied, "Amazing! What sort of curse?" The woman sighed and replied, "Mr. Heppleworth!"

Some may feel just like this about ministry. It's here, it's new, it's brilliant but, oh, the curse! The curse of all those things we've seen in the last two chapters. It seems that the whole enterprise may not be worth it. Or, at least we're not sure where we're going with it or where to start. So, in this chapter, we turn a corner somewhat. We're offering three foundational building blocks on which to rest a more firm and a more collaborative ministry. These three blocks are: community, servanthood, and formation. On these blocks we hope to erect in the following chapters a stable edifice of practical shared ministry.

Before we see the relevance of our first building block, community, we are instantly aware that in many parts of our country, community is more an ideal than a reality. For one thing, we North Americans are forever caught in a peculiar tradition of high individualism as over and against communal living. Our folk heroes are loners who move in to town, do their thing, and then ride off into the sunset. Our exaltation of individualism has reached its peak in what Tom Wolfe has dubbed the "me generation." A proliferation of I'm-My-Own-Best-Friend books and the like have given ample and multi-million dollar testimony to the persistence of individualism. Add to this our high mobility, our constant change of address, and you can see how elusive community is. And yet, ambiguity remains. As Daniel Yankelovich has stated in his survey,

> Among the people I interviewed, many truly committed self-fulfillment seekers, focus so sharply on their own needs that instead of achieving the more intimate relationships they desire, they grow farther apart from others. In dwelling on their own needs they discover that the inner journey brings loneliness and depression.... Americans are learning from their life experiments that self-absorption is not a sound strategy....[1]

If community is always an uphill goal for highly individualized and mobile Americans, then it is also made more difficult by our actual church structures. There is no doubt that the church most of us are used to, a church mediated through large parish plants and complex, multi-officed chanceries, is like that of an established, huge corporation. But, a look backward to the New Testament times reveals a Christian religion composed of small voluntary relationships. As we saw before, the first shape this took was that of the Jewish-Christian congregation gathered around the twelve apostles. But then, as Moltmann points out, there was a momentous decision to expand this circle to include non-Jews. Therefore there evolved the mixed fellowship of Jews and Gentiles. The term *Christian Church* was first coined at Antioch in Syria, Palestine's neighbor, for such a joined congregation. The mixture was a potent way of saying that the church was indeed an open community and it offered personal communal fellowship to all.

This is in contrast to the impersonal forces of greed and self-centered individualism of the empire.

In the fourth century, there was another momentous decision made, the decision to let Christianity become the public state religion and therefore a part of the public order. As we might expect, it was not very long before the new religion went from a small voluntary group of believers without boundaries to a large organization following the Roman political patterns of districts, regions, and provinces. Such concepts were easily translated into parishes, dioceses, and national conferences. Since such districts were based on geography and not on voluntary fellowships, then roles changed considerably. The ministry of the clergy took on the character of civil authority and became abstracted from the common, local community. Ministry and service were rerouted as public welfare and private charity came to the fore. The living word, the sacraments, were transmitted into objects to be given, handed down, administered by the clergy. The local congregation was changed into an organizational subdivision whose autonomy was subsumed by the next higher level or organization. Ministry became a vertical thing, not something necessarily shared by and offered to the local disciples horizontally.

Things were neither so simple nor so deliberate as might be suggested by this survey. After all, organization certainly was necessary as large numbers came into the church for whatever reason. It's just that, as happens so often, largeness can subvert a sense of community and induce a certain powerlessness on the local level. It easily happens that the large, over-all general office takes on the whole identity of the widespread corporation and does the thinking and deciding for it. This is what happened to the church, especially in those high medieval times of Roman centralization under the jurist, or legal-minded, popes. So some are saying that if we are ever to form a really authentic church, establish community, and promote genuine ministries, we must take the excessive attention off the national or international headquarters and refocus once more on the local congregation. We would do this, but not in the sense that we do not acknowledge the very real communion each congregation has with every other; not in the sense that the realities of an institutional church are not both valid and needful; not in the sense, as we pointed out in the last chapter, that we lose our concept of universality. We would do this because of the conviction that real renewal of community is a grass roots affair, and that ministry, which starts from the ground up rather than being imposed from the top, has a better chance of integration. We refocus on the local congregation because of the conviction that it is there that the clergy are going to reenter as fellow parishioners and that fellow parishioners can co-minister with them. Both products of the local scene, clergy and laity have a better chance to promote the genius and gifts that the local culture offers and demands.

It should be obvious that if we are offering renewed attention to the local congregation (for most, the local parish), we are only going back to our apostolic roots. Then, as we saw, community determined the ministries and not the other way. There the ministries and offices that emerged and mutated were always measured as to authenticity and validity against service to the community. And, of course, this is why our current inherited form of office such as that of bishop, presbyter, and deacon is always capable of being transcended. By focusing on the local community, we are realizing priorities and indicating that such communities will not so much receive ministers as spawn them. And time will tell if such new ministries that may arise from the roots will be integrated into the current superstructure (such as the prophets and teachers were absorbed into the episcopacy or the Franciscans into a religious order) or remain in tension with the hierarchy.

A strong sense of identity, of belonging to the same community, of being responsible for one another, and of always being under the judgment of the gospel, made the first Christian gatherings ideal. There is no question they promoted many ministries and celebrated a variety of gifts. By giving close scrutiny to our local congregations, by renewing the life of the parish,[2] by seeing ourselves "planted where we are," we have a better chance to overcome the tensions that arise as people, cleric and lay, come together in the name of the Lord.

This focus on the community is in fact receiving some strong emphasis from an unexpected quarter: the proposed new code of Canon Law that is to be implemented in 1983. The new code proposes a definite reversal of the medieval concept of seeing the local parish primarily in terms of the priest. Rather, it puts full attention on the community of people who remain as over and against the priest who may come and go. This is a radical change and obviously reflects Vatican II's understanding of the church as the people of God and the fact that there are not enough priests to fill the world's parishes. The result of this new focus is that the new code fosters some creative ways of dealing with priestless parishes, namely through the legitimizing of many lay ministerial options. While it remains to be seen how all this works out in practice, we should not fail to note that the new code has taken history seriously and returned to the basic community and its needs as the starting point of ministry.

—2—

Our second building block is the concept of the servant-leader. Avery Dulles has given us five models of the church, models that were all interdependent and quite descriptive of our identity as the people of God. Later, however, he added another model or rather one that catches the best of all the others. He calls us a "community of disciples." A disciple implies that one is a pilgrim, is still trying to comprehend, still learning. To be a disciple is also to be under authority and correction, on the way to full conversion. To be a disciple in a whole community of disciples implies mutual concern and mutual ministry in the name of the master who binds all together with his Spirit. In this model, the genuine leader is the one who is the best disciple. The best disciple is the one who best imitates Jesus who acted as servant and washed the feet of all. In other words, real authority and leadership, the real roots of Christian ministry, are to be found here. As Robert Greenleaf expresses it in his remarkable book, *Servant Leadership:*

> A new moral principle is emerging which holds that the only authority deserving of one's allegiance is that which is freely and knowingly granted by the led to the leader in response to, and in proportion to, the clearly evident servant stature of the leader. Those who choose to follow this principle will not casually accept the authority of existing institutions. *Rather, they will freely respond only to individuals who are chosen as leaders because they are proven and trusted as servants.* To the extent that this principle prevails in the future, the only truly viable institutions will be those that are predominantly servant-led (italics added).[3]

Perhaps our institution of the church has not been viable because its image is so much that of power, unilateral authority, and master-led. In this regard, Robert Greenleaf has some interesting comments. Someone asked him to assess the situation of the Catholic Church in America and he gave an answer that applied to it and to some of the other churches. He said that the Catholic Church is potentially the largest single force for good in the country, but it fails to reach such a potential because it is projected in such negative terms. People know with clarity and precision what the Catholic Church is *against* (for example, birth control, abortion, divorce, and so on) but not what the church is *for,* at least not with the same clarity and precision. People do not know unambiguously what the Catholic Church truly, enduringly, and conscientiously affirms as the very essence of its being, the very reason for its existence. They do not identify the church with healing, reconciliation, or service, although, in fact, there are daily incredible acts of all three. Unlike the Quakers, for example, who are known for peace efforts and the abolition of slavery, the Catholic Church has no such positive image. Pomp and circumstance, movie cardinals, and television palaces are what is projected by a biased world. No one thinks automatically of the poor Foot-Washer of Nazareth when he or she thinks of the Catholic Church. Greenleaf, a non-Catholic, mentions the impact of Pope John XXIII as one who, in fact, did signify the best for which a church should stand.

All this puts the local congregation under judgment. As we struggle to clarify the roles of ministry, too often we are in reality struggling for power. There has to be a profound understanding of and conviction about ministry as being fundamentally servant-hood, if conflicts are to be resolved. The notion of the servant-leader is probably the only solid ground on which to build ministry, the only way that clergy and laity are going to come to terms.

It is obvious that the question of servant-leadership is one that the priest, in the present state of things, must be sensitive to in a special way. He is a leader and has been since time immemorial. He will continue to be in the future, for it is his charism. For him, then, leadership becomes a question of style and how he perceives his role. He can see it in the more recent tradition of authority-over-all or in the older tradition of servanthood. Liturgist John Gallen harkens to the old formula when he writes, "The priest is to lead the eucharistic assembly because it is the priest's role to be servant-leader of the community."[4] The more this approach is understood, the more the servant role-model is appropriated, the more readily will the priest change his style, and questions of authority, cooperation, and obedience will be resolved in this light.

There is, by the way, an allied theological insight that bears on this issue. In the old theology, the priest at Mass was perceived as standing in the place of Christ himself. It is he who utters the august words of consecration in direct discourse: "This is my body.... This is my blood." He consecrates and, at this moment above all, he alone is the "Christ." As Pius XII said while talking to the delegates of the First International Congress on Pastoral Liturgy in 1956, "Therefore it is the priest celebrant, and he alone who, putting on the person of Christ, sacrifices; not the people, nor the clerics, nor even the priests who reverently assist." But against this rather exclusive emphasis, more recent theologians would point out that there is, in our Western tradition, really an implicit calling down of the Holy Spirit. The reading of the eucharistic prayers shows this. Therefore it is the Holy Spirit that has the active role in the consecration. The Eastern liturgies are even more explicit on this score. This may seem an esoteric comment until you realize the subtle shift in the priest's role, namely, a shift from his traditional role of the one acting solely in the person of Christ as Pius XII indicates. His role might be seen more accurately as one of representative of the church, the community, as he calls for the coming of the Holy Spirit. His role, therefore, is far more community oriented and invites the fundamental participation of all. In other words, in this view, his role moves subtly away from that of chief actor to that of chief servant.

In any case, the rather constant imagery both derived from scripture and from tradition is that of servant-leader and so this must pervade the priest's vision of his role and authority. We are, of course, at a point of history when his role, overly inflated from the uncritical excess of the past, is being deflated. It's a painful process for both clergy and laity. Still, no amount of priestly demythologizing or deflating will cancel his basic community presidency. As we keep insisting, it is his style that must change. It must be his understanding that power in the church is intimately related to servanthood, that powerlessness from the cross is still the most powerful invitation to obedience. Henri Nouwen's reflection is helpful.

> . . . real ministers, real servants, are powerless. They cannot even decide how to be servants. If training and formation are valuable, it is not because they offer us some power, but because they lead us to powerless availability. To be a minister is to be without power.... Ministers do not even have the power of knowledge. Their years of study only lead them to the humble awareness of the inscrutable mystery of God and to the ever-deepening realization that in God's presence they can only stutter, or better, be silent....

> Whenever we use the Word and the Sacrament to exercise power we betray our vocation.... If Word and Sacrament could be removed from the realm of professional tools, and experienced as participation in the humbling way of Christ, laymen and laywomen, sisters and brothers, deacons, priests and bishops might find it much easier to enter into a creative dialogue about the many ways in which the presence of the powerless Christ could be made visible in the daily life of the church.[5]

—3—

From the beginning, the community of the local parish evokes the ministries that will best serve its needs. The ministers who respond do so as servants of the community. The leader is leader because he or she qualifies as most faithful servant. So far so good. But another factor is needed if we are to resolve the tensions within ministry. Another building block is required—formation. An old moral theology professor of mine, who taught little moral but much old Yankee wisdom, used to say that the worse combination in the world is lots of pep and no judgment. There's much truth here. Good will is not enough. There must be some backgrounding, some training, some formation. There must be some informal, or nowadays, formal schooling to acquire the necessary skills to minister. There must be formation.

The trouble is that formation is a worrisome word. No matter how you try, it carries with it a taint of elitism: of being better educated, better read, better trained, better in prayer life. People who have gone through formation, especially in degreed programs in universities or theology seminars do tend to dialogue only with those "of their own kind." They do tend to fall into jargon and use the "in" words of their discipline. They easily get out of touch with the common person. And this, of course, is deadly to real community where people from the highways and byways are the constituents of the "community of disciples." Still, the fact is that formative intellectual and technical skills are needed in today's world. On the other hand, this makes it more imperative than ever that trained and degreed ministers concentrate on the servant-leader mode. This, in turn, is a way of saying that the essential and critical foundation of all formation is spirituality. A profound sense of service, of washing of the feet is the only way to keep ourselves humble, and, literally and figuratively "in touch" with all the people.

Spirituality concentrates on the *why:* why we are doing ministry, why we are motivated, and why we were chosen. Alfred Hughes says:

> As we explore the possibilities of the present moment in church history, it becomes clearer that the sound of spiritual maturation of potential church ministries is extremely central. The role of the church is not just to multiply service to others. It is further the redemptive mission of Jesus Christ.... This understanding of church ministry means that those who enter it must have grown in sufficient depth in faith and moral living to be able to help others do the same. They must be moving into greater communion with God, a deeper conversion of heart, a more expansive charity and a more mature love for the church.... It is spiritual maturity that draws others to maturity in their lives. It is holiness that attracts others to a holy way of life.[6]

Lay ministry is, as we have indicated so often, mission oriented, based on the Lord's impulse to "baptize all nations," to be a living sign, to be a saint. Nikos Kazantzakis tells of his visit to a monastery in Crete in a time of intense spiritual searching. "It was Father Joachim who, clapping his hands as though I was a pullet, shooed me away. 'Return to the world,' he cried. 'In this day and age the world is the true monastery and that is where you will become a saint.' "[7] This is the real call to ministry: to open our lives so that they may be used, like Christ's, to heal the world's pain and suffering. To this extent, ministry is never really something we do, but rather the response to those gifts each of us has been given.

The fundamental formation about which we are speaking is a spiritual formation. We need guidance in getting in touch with the depth of our own lives, to discover what God is already doing there. We learn to listen, to respond, to meditate, to see our own lives in interconnectedness with all of creation, to be familiar with the great spiritual masters, to pray and to find resurrection through the cross. It is only when ministers, ordained and non-ordained, tap into the gospel roots together that there is any possibility of working out the perplexing relationships between them that exist now. (At least, it's an essential starting place for the dialogue to begin.) It is only when ministers, ordained and non-ordained, tap into the gospel roots together that Christian servanthood, ministry, and community are possible.

Beyond this, to speak of further formation is to talk about quite important but commonplace things that need not detain us here: the conviction that professionalism is necessary in full time ministry, the availability of ongoing education, the prioritizing of the parish budget to allow for learning opportunities, a mechanism for certification and placement, the deep grounding in the Catholic tradition. The latter is to be noted.

Theresa Monroe, a perceptive lay minister, comments about some ministers whose convictions are not filtered through the traditions and teaching of the church:

> I had an example of this a few weeks ago. I stayed with a woman who is a wonderful person. She had been hired by her parish to supervise the religious education program. Her brother was also visiting her and he had not been to church in years, but was planning to go to church that Sunday morning because she was involved in the planning of the liturgy. She told him, "Now I want you to feel free to go to communion. The old rules have changed and the church doesn't require confession any more. Don't worry about it." I thought to myself, "I'm not sure that's what I would want my children to be taught in a religious education program!"[8]

She is right. The tradition has to be better served than that. The person handing on the tradition has to be better formed and informed than that. As Sallie McFague of the Vanderbilt Divinity School points out, "A person must get inside a religious tradition, be able to move around in it both comfortably and critically, love it and question it at the same time.... This is what formation is about

—the settling of a religious tradition into the very flesh and bones of one's existence."⁹

Many have read the moving little book, *I Heard the Owl Call My Name.* It's the story of a young minister who has a terminal illness. His doctors estimate that he has about two years to live, maybe three. They do not tell him this news but they do tell his bishop. The bishop sends the young clergyman to the most difficult and remote parish in the entire diocese. There he begins to minister to the native Indians. In this hard ministry, he finds himself confronting the simple and fundamental things in life. All the superficial, petty concerns are stripped away. He immerses himself in his ministry and spends a great deal of his time in helping the young Indian people get a half way decent start in life. The parish is flourishing but the young minister's health is failing. Finally, his bishop comes to visit him. The bishop talks about his own life and why this particular corner of the diocese has meant so much to him. He says, "It has been easier here, where only the fundamentals count, to learn that thing which every person has to learn before they leave this earth...." And the young minister asks, "What is that?" The bishop replies, "Enough of the meaning of life is to be ready to die."

This story gathers in a moving way our three building blocks to make ministry work, to make cooperation work. It tells us of local community, it tells us of the powerless servanthood of the minister (and therefore his success), it tells us of his spiritual formation. The story gives us enough of the meaning of ministry to help us to die to isolation, power, and shallowness, the opposite qualities of our ministerial foundations.

Naturally there shall remain conflict in the assembly and perhaps a parting good word should be said for conflict, for it too is an authentic dynamic in community life. Without it there is no advancement, no growth, and so conflict is quite appropriate for a community of disciples. And, truth to tell, it's been there from the very beginning as even a casual reading of the New Testament will verify. Ultimately, conflict can be a creative force. It can be one of the livelier elements that cement community, servanthood, and formation together.

CHAPTER EIGHT

The Parish

—1—

George Washington Carver, the Black scientist who achieved such wonders with the lowly peanut, liked to tell this story. "When I was young I said to God. 'God, tell me the mystery of the universe.' But God answered, 'That knowledge is reserved for me alone.' So I said, 'God, tell me the mystery of the peanut.' Then God said, 'Well, George, that's more nearly your size.' And he told me." That's a good story for the point I would like to make here.

Ideally, it would be fitting to take all of the data from the past pages and explore in depth the manifold theological applications of ministry on a great, universal cosmic scale. But that is beyond me. That is knowledge reserved for someone else. My more modest focus is more peanut-like, on something I've known all my life: the parish. So, for the rest of this book, we will explore ministry's practical expressions in relation to the parish moving from some overview statements in this chapter to the very practical applications in the next. This is not to slight the other important and viable forms of Christian community from covenant groupings to campus ministries. It is just that for the average Catholic, especially in the formative years, the parish remains the focal point of faith, growth, and celebration. And, for all of the vast changes in the church and society it will likely remain so, even in an increasingly secular world.

When we speak of an increasingly secular world, we mean the pervasive loss of the Jewish-Christian symbols, the drastic drop-off of church attendance, especially among the young, and the powerlessness we all feel before the global onslaught of anti-Christian values so well packaged and publicized by the multimedia powers. So successful is this secularism that sociologist Peter Berger claims that by the end of the century the committed Christian will be like a Tibetan monk on campus—someone respected, a curiosity, but hardly mattering.

All this bespeaks a growing and vast indifferentism to organized religion. According to George Gallup and David Poling in their book, *The Search for America's Faith,*[1] many are not really hostile to organized religion; they just find it irrelevant. They like to cite the low level of spirituality they find in most churches; massive interest in busy work, buildings, and money; and, they add, the church's seeming immunity to society's real social problems and the needs of the poor and the marginal. Others' interests are so absorbed by a whole series of "lifestyles" and mobility that, as in the parable, nothing can take root.

Still something else shows up. Gallop's respondents among the unchurched indicated by a margin of 52 percent that they could foresee the possibility of becoming a fairly active member in a church

> if they could find a pastor or church friends with whom they could easily and openly discuss their religious doubts.... This group also said that they would like to openly discuss their spiritual needs with a church leader or congregational member.... Some 14 percent of the unchurched were emphatic about finding a church that not only had good preaching but also is seriously concerned to work for a better society.[2]

There is hope then, and, to many, the most public outreach to fulfill this hope is the parish. Gallup goes on to say:

> While many Christian sociologists fear the inroads of the mass media because the media project the electric church as a pleasant, armchair substitute for real life Christianity, others believe that the future battle for a meaningful spiritual life will be won or lost in the local

parish.... As Christian people regain their vision of the universal
church, they will discover that the local congregation and its surrounding, sustaining, parish is where Christ chooses to greet and sus-
tain us. It is truly impossible to love and honor the church universal
before we have loved and supported the church in our house, as Saint
Paul describes it.[3]

So the parish remains one of the more viable places of hope
and potential in our secular society. As such, it has been the object
of recent studies. The bishops of the United States have set up a
commission called the National Conference of Catholic Bishops'
Parish Project with Reverend Phil Murnion as its director. He and
his staff have done considerable research and have surfaced the
following national concerns about the parish. Based on the studies
of Andrew Greeley and others, the report, entitled *What Do People
Want?*, enumerates the following points, which I have para-
phrased. People want:

1. Liturgies that nourish their faith and, above all, good sermons
   that do the same.
2. That the parish have as its agenda everyday practical concerns:
   family life, children, teens, etc.
3. A democratic form of leadership.
4. The parish should be an alive and dynamic place.
5. Priests should be able to work well with others.
6. There should be a sense of community.
7. There should be opportunity to develop spiritually.
8. There must be care for people who are hurting.

If these are the concerns, research from this same group
found that the country's most effective parishes to meet these needs
were those which (1) provided organizational activities such as
adult education, liturgical planning, youth ministry, help to the
elderly and (2) had a definite pattern of shared responsibility and
ministry. The qualities that showed up as conducive to such effec-
tiveness were: (1) many opportunities for the people to participate
in the parish, (2) the quality of the parish staff, and (3) the overall
vision of the parish.

As long as we're into cataloging, this research team also surfaced what they call the ingredients for parish renewal:

1. Participatory leadership
2. Awareness of people needs
3. A clear sense of priorities
4. More people being trained to participate sensibly (formation)
5. Personal commitment to Christ and the church
6. The opportunities to meet in small groups
7. Attentiveness to relationships, especially to the male-female ones in ministry
8. The enablement of all to minister to one another
9. The availability of resources

It is obvious that many of these items in all listings are popular translations of the Vatican II's principles of collegiality, shared responsibility, and an emphasis on the baptismal rights of the people of God. It is likewise obvious that, perhaps unknowingly, these are popular street expressions of much of the history we have seen in the previous chapters.

—2—

Many of the comments listed above find an excellent practical summary in Australian Peter Rudge's thesis, which goes like this: that the way a local church organizes its common life says far more about what it believes than all that it teaches and preaches.[4] It is one thing to talk about shared ministry, enablement, a parish of people, and all that, and quite another to create an organizational style that makes it possible for these things to take place. Rudge then goes on to analyze what he calls five styles of parish—none pure, most mixed—and gives us a brief description along with strengths and weaknesses of each mode. It will be instructive to review them. Also, as we go through them, we might think of our own parish.

1. *Traditional Style.* The description here is the parish which sees its primary task as the transmission of the heritage. It tends therefore to be rather non-reflective, hierarchial, with most of its energy going towards maintaining the *status quo*. The *strength* of this style of parish is that it provides people with a great sense of security, a sense of being in touch with the good old days, a sense of

being rooted. And today this is no small thing. As "lifestyles" even in religion abound, as yesterday's vices are today's virtues and *vice versa,* as everything seems to becoming "unglued," this style has appeal.

These are the people who are deeply hurt, for they sent their children to the parochial school as directed, then to the Catholic high school, and then to the Catholic college, and the children have graduated as certified atheists. These are the people who feel profoundly betrayed by a shift of emphasis and rules upon which they based their religious lives, now to find themselves standing on shakey ground, if there is any ground left at all. These are the people buffeted by the "do your own thing" and "follow your own conscience" school. These are the people who look with dismay at the rootlessness of youth, their high suicide rate, and their complaints about life being meaningless. These are the ones who react in horror to the reports that the average young adult is a religious illiterate, who couldn't name half of the twelve apostles on a bet and are even surprised to learn that there are twelve. The traditional style of parish, therefore, serves the deep needs of the many people. It has its *weakness,* of course, and it's a serious one: it cuts off new sources of vitality and growth. It simply does not provide for any kind of enabling ministry, since it keeps all authority and power in the hands of the clergy.

2. *Charismatic* or *Intuitive Style.*   This style revolves around the personality of the pastor. It tends to be prophetic, strongly rejecting the *status quo,* and instead very much open to initiative and spontaneity. Its *strength* is precisely its vitality and its flexibility. This style of parish appeals to the more "liberated" who enjoys such aliveness and likes to let things "happen," who knows that experimentation in liturgy and prayer forms will be appreciated and welcome, who is at home with colorful banners as well as traditional statues. The *weakness* here is that such a parish, revolving around the gifted personality of its leader, might well rise or fall with his transfer. Many have seen that; a parish can do a real turnabout when the pastor goes or comes. Secondly, such a parish does tend to be somewhat judgmental in character, centering around those who are the "in" people and those who are "out." But mostly, as we said, there is a too heavy dependence on the leader.

3. *Classic Style.*   This is hierarchial, highly relational, and heavily dependent on the delegation of authority. Each person fits into a ready-made structure inherited from the past. This style of parish, be it noted, can be quite innovative but it is understood that, even here, everything happens within the structure system. The *strength* of this style of parish is efficiency and speed. Also, and this is critical, everyone knows where he or she stands. There is no ambiguity whatever in the chain of command, delegation, or where the buck stops. It's a neat system that is rightly appealing to many, allowing innovation while being protected by a well-defined delegation and structure system. But this too is its *weakness.* The structure tends to shape the response and so limits vitality and interdependence. That is, you must go through channels even with a new idea, and the new idea will take the form of the structure and can't go beyond it. Since you must always go through channels, this is tough on the prophetic and charismatic, since it is limiting to the creative person. But, most of all, it creates too much dependency.

Sociologist Gerald Eagan tells the story of a man who jumped into the river to save someone from drowning as the bystanders cheered him on. A little later he jumped into the river a second time to save another drowning person. More cheers. He did this three, four, five, eight, ten times. He turned his back on the bystanders and began walking upstream. Suddenly the bystanders saw another man drowning and they called out to their hero for help. When he ignored their pleas and continued walking on, they accused him of indifference and negligence. But he turned to them and said, "Save him yourselves. I'm going upstream to find out whose throwing all these people in!" The classic style of parish carries the moral of this story.

4. *Human Relations Style.*   Here the emphasis is on the personal. The style in this parish is nondirective as the psychologists say. There is developed here a great team spirit and intimate relations among the staff. Promoted are group development, a high degree of personal satisfaction, and a real feeling of commitment. It's a good place to be. It's a great feeling. The *strength* of this style parish is obvious: there is a strong sense of support. One is never alone. One belongs to a team with whom relating is easy, whether it's Father or Sister or the DRE. There's a feeling of being backed

up all the way. The *weakness* here is predictable: there can be too much "ingroupness." A clique mentality can develop. But more than this, the team spirit can be so good, the feeling of commitment so high, that who would be willing to rock the boat with some issues that are a little touchy? In short, at times the pressure needed to maintain harmony causes some really basic issues to be suppressed. Such issues will come out sooner or later, but then explosively.

5. *Systemic Style.* This is an interesting style. Its high motif is interdependency and the capacity to meet changing needs. There is a leader here, all right, the pastor, but his function is radically different from, say, that of the pastors of the traditional style parish. This pastor does not do ministry as much because he helps others to identify and carry out their own ministries, which are uniquely theirs in virtue of baptism. Here the various people relate to one another in interdependency for common objectives. The *strength* here is the emphasis on shared authority and mutual ministry, leading the people from dependency to real interdependency. Not independency notice, but *inter*dependency—a real respect for each person's gifts and a sense of common objective and goals toward which each may strive. Here each is mindful of his or her own gifts yet at the same time conscious of community. The *weakness* is that this style of parish is hard to sell to the average congregation. People have been trained, like the priest himself, that Father is universal practitioner of all things whatever. They too have been loaded with the expectations of the priest's role that are quite unreal. They want him to "be all things to all men" (and women). They do not want a "second fiddle" lector or eucharistic minister giving them communion or a layperson visiting them at the hospital. They want the man who was ordained to be always available. Another weakness in this systemic style of parish is that you can forge a gap between those people of the congregation who do want the traditional roles intact and the elite who are the ministering people, quite happy with the new role of sharing.

—3—

No one parish is likely to be a perfect example of any style described above, but maybe that's not so much the point. The point is that it is the last style parish, the systemic, that Vatican II and the documents of our own bishops seem to be leading us to as an ideal. In their annual message, *Called and Gifted: Catholic Laity,* the bishops say very systemic things as:

> While focusing on the laity we wish to address the whole church. We affirm the vision of the Second Vatican Council and the importance it gives to the laity ... thanks to the impetus of the Second Vatican Council, laywomen and men feel themselves called to exercise the same mature interdependence and practical self-direction which characterize them in other areas of life.... The adult character of the people of God flows from baptism and confirmation.... Baptism and confirmation empower all believers to share in some form of ministry.... This unity of ministry should be especially evident in the relationships between laity and clergy as laymen and women respond to the call of the Spirit in their lives. The clergy help to call forth, identify, coordinate and affirm the diverse gifts bestowed by the Spirit....

This seems to be a clear call to a more shared kind of parish life and responsibility, whether we call this style "systemic" or not. It also seems to tell us that we are being pushed back into primitive roles where several gifts were appreciated and the priest was in the much wider posture of community leader rather than the more narrow one which bound him almost exclusively to the altar. Some, of course, find this both threatening and downgrading and full of ambiguity. One such critic writes:

> The net result of such deliberate ambiguity is to reduce the priesthood to merely another among many "ministries." More and more this attitude diminishes the incredible difference between priest and people, even in the presence of a healthy new partnership. More and more the priest is situated as a kind of scoutmaster, *primus inter pares,* rather than as someone unbelievably gifted with the very power to confect his God daily.[5]

One has to be sympathetic to such expressions, but maybe one should also see them as part of the pain of realigning both the parish community and ministry. The pain is partly caused also by the fact that we are so far from reaching our goals, that we are still in the throes of moving away from an excessive clericalism to a more fraternal and shared giftedness. But we must continue, for it is this shared giftedness of ministry that directs us to the parish envisioned by Vatican II.

In this whole context, Peter Rudge speaks of several principles to guide the community's pastor. First, he says, it is more important for the ordained to enable others to identify and carry out their missions than to do it themselves. Secondly, the ordained must be convinced that interdependency is always preferable to dependency so that everything does not stand or fall with the pastor. Thirdly, he suggests that the greatest gift that any pastor (or minister) can give to another is not the right answer but the authenticity of his or her own search. As Westerhoff and Willimon say, the minister "must not take other Christians' ministry away from them, or allow them to give their ministry to their priests. The role of the priest is to illumine, equip, support, confirm, serve, and symbolize the ministry of all his or her fellow Christians, not to take their ministry upon his or her shoulders."[6]

These are the ideals of parish and ministry working in harmony. Such analyses, as we have been doing, however, should not blind us to larger issues, issues that go beyond the tactics of ordained and non-ordained ministry. Whatever style we prefer, however many interdependent ministries we have, there still is the spiritual focus to deal with. There is the spiritual formation that forces us to remember that no parish, of whatever style, is designed to be a comfortable island of wall-to-wall safety. The parish is no place to come for a comfortable social life or those exciting activities and programs that console our consciences (we are, after all, *doing* something). It is no place to cater to our sense of well-being. It should be more than that. The parish must be there to create space where we are face to face with our true pain, know our sinfulness and consequently our need for God's grace and mercy. Henri Nouwen has seized on the problem well. He says:

A comfortable space is created which is filled up with sermons, activities, projects. But what if a minister encouraged people to listen to God? To listen to each other? My sense is that if *that* happened, people would suddenly feel much more in touch with themselves, with God and with the world. They would hear clearly what their particular vocation is, where they are called to serve.... You see, the trouble with a lot of service is that a lot of projects are designed to make *us* feel good. But a real service that comes out of our experience of God's presence in our life and his grace and mercy, and my wish to communicate that—that service presupposes a willingness to confront myself, and in the self-confrontation to discover God.[7]

If we take these words to heart and make such a discovery of God, we are more likely to bear witness, a witness that, like our Master's, does not necessarily end in success, and the parish must be prepared for that. There's a story about Mother Teresa—I don't know if it's true or not—that fits well here. Some reporters were interviewing her and her work in Calcutta. One reporter was dismayed at the countless people in the streets needing help. He looked at Mother Teresa, waved his arms at the vast expanse of suffering humanity, and said in desperation, "Mother Teresa, this is an impossible task! You simply cannot help all these people. You can't possibly hope to be successful!" And Mother Teresa, tapping his chest with her bony finger, said, "Young man, we are not here to be successful. We are here to be faithful." A good motto for the parish that has discovered God.

I think there's one final thought about the parish that must be said aloud. The parish *is* a place to confront oneself, one's pain, one's God. It *is* a place that must bear faithful witness. But it is also a place where many Christs must be accepted and welcomed and even ministered to, as in their own way they minister to us. Perhaps no one has caught this theme more poignantly than Will Campbell in his marvelous book, *Brother to a Dragonfly*. Will Campbell, a Baptist minister, is that "dangerous combination" of a Southerner and a civil rights advocate. It's in the 60's and his sister's son has died. He has promised to sit up all night at the wake. He's sitting in the parlor with the body, thinking he's all alone.

"Believe it's cooled off a bit." "Yea, I believe it has." Slowly the realization encompassed me that someone from out of the darkness, six or eight rows behind, had spoken to me. And I had answered. I did not need to turn around to ask the identity of the speaker. I had not heard that voice for a long time. But I know it was that of a favorite uncle of our childhood days. In recent years he had been one of the most critical and vocal ones concerning my activities in the civil rights and desegregation controversy, expressing bitter disappointment and displeasure that his own nephew had turned out to be a nigger lover and renegade preacher. I had ceased to visit him when I came because I loved him too much to risk rejection. He was the one uncle who would never, and he did never, *join the church.* At revival time he was always the prime subject for conversion teams. While lesser men would offer excuses of how they knew there were hypocrites in church they were just as good as, or allow that they could worship God in their own backyard, he always listened politely to the evangelistic pitch, thanked the caller but offered no explanation or promise regarding his recalcitrance. It was considered strange behavior.

He moved quietly out of the darkness and sat down beside me. I glanced at my watch. "It's three o'clock," he said, I assumed that he knew of the promise I had made my sister, and had been sitting in the shadows since the last mourner had left, deciding in his own time and in his own mind when I had been alone—though not alone—long enough.

He poured coffee from a lunch box thermos and handed it to me. Until the dawn I sat in the redemptive company of a racist Jesus.[8]

Ministers come in strange garb. Not all are officially appointed, installed, or recognized. Not all are even good people. Yet, somehow, the parish must give space to them too, for some day, some way, just when we need it most, the worst will minister their best and suddenly we'll recognize even a "racist Christ" among us.

CHAPTER NINE

The Real World

—1—

When the Velveteen Rabbit asked his famous question, "What is Real?" he must have had books like this in mind. There's theory and there's ideal concerning ministry, mutual sharing, cooperation and collaboration. But down in the parish trenches, "What is Real?" is the common question. And the answer, whether we like it or not, is pretty much the response of the old Skin Horse to whom this question was first addressed. He replied that Real is a thing that happens; it takes a long time, *and* there's pain involved. That's why, to paraphrase the Skin Horse, it doesn't often happen to parishes or ministers who break easily (for whom life is full of problems, not mysteries) or have sharp edges (sarcasm will get you nowhere), or who have to be carefully kept (buildings before people: "This gym will be open from 10:00 a.m. to 11:00 a.m. daily"). Generally, as the Skin Horse reminds us, by the time you're Real, most of your hair has been loved off ("Have I been DRE that long?"), and your eyes drop out ("You know, I can't see a thing anymore without my glasses."), and you get loose in the joints ("It's those damn nursing homes that don't have elevators!") and very shabby ("Father needs a haircut again." or "This room really needs a paint job."). But eventually, in spite of such wear and tear, becoming Real does happen to parishes and ministers who are willing to take on the slow process of opening themselves to the Spirit. Real happens at the end of long (and sometimes painful) shared experiences, which is the essence of community. Real is the end product of many ministries, many gifts, that fall into place.

But, back to our question: what *is* Real for the average parish in the area of ministry? How does it happen? Or, to put it another way, are there really down-to-earth, practical translations of the systemic parish, of many gifts at work? Are there parishes which have experiences that we can draw on so we can get started? The answer is yes, there are, and the number of such parishes is growing every day. Some have even recorded their journeys from old-time to new-time parishes. Such a one is Msgr. Robert Fuller in his book, *Adventures of a Collegial Parish* (Mystic, Ct.: Twenty-Third Publications). There are creative and imaginative parishes catalogued and written up by Reverend Phil Murnion in nationally syndicated columns, and in his *Parish Ministry* newsletter (New York: William H. Sadlier, Inc.). There are a growing number of helping programs and staffs dedicated to making unreal parishes Real. Such would be Father Tom Sweester's Parish Evaluation Project in Chicago or Father Blaine Barr's work in Minneapolis and Brother Loughlan Sofield's Ministries Center for the Laity in Brooklyn, N.Y., and the National Institute for Lay Training in New York City. So we are not without examples, not without assistance. But meanwhile, while we track down such sources, we can offer some practical examples ourselves in the following pages. Such examples are not exhaustive, they are only partial samplings of ministerial opportunities. I suggest you study the examples from our Parish Booklet in the appendix for an overview of the type of ministries and the scope of involvement. Meanwhile the following illustrations may be of some help.

The basic fears of the laity, you may recall, on considering ministry are a lack of self-confidence, apprehension of being consumed by it, and a sense of unworthiness. To overcome such fears and to induce many to ministry, our parish uses the Triple Approach which has been quite successful. First of all, we seek out by personal contact (letter, phone call, or face-to-face) a host couple (or individual or friends) who will be in charge of a particular activity for the year. To soften the reaction we quickly add the second part: we remind the people that this is a one-shot deal. Let's take an example. Each year we have a lenten communal confession, very lovely and moving with darkness and candlelight as powerful symbols of the movement from the darkness of sin to the light of forgiveness. It happens one night. Then it's over. No matter how reluctant or unconfident a couple may be, the thought that it will all be over, that it is a one-shot affair, is quite sustaining. But then there's the third part of the Triple Approach—what we call the piggyback part. This means that *last* year's couple will be there with them to help them share their past experience and train them along the way. The new couple, in turn, is committed to training next year's couple.

In the beginning, of course, I have had to spend a lot of time in training, giving the theology, the new approaches, the reasons for changes. There were lectures, books, articles, bulletin flyers, and all the rest. But gradually all this paid off. The first couple was able to pass on the teachings to their successors and right on down the line from year to year. In the meantime, a little folder was being collected containing all the details, a log of what actually took place from year to year to year, and recording the resources needed for a particular event. A tradition, in other words, was forming. What we're seeing here in this particular example is a general soft approach to the beginning of ministry: calling the person or persons, giving them a manageable task for a one-time event, and backing them up with the experienced support and encouragement of the previous couple. The side effects are equally valuable. People get to meet new people; they get an easy introduction to ministry, acquire some self-confidence, and often are ready for more sustained ministries. There is training (formation), ready-measured success, and exposure to the larger community.

There is one other unspoken factor operating here. It is the role of the pastor. Here is where the charism of leadership is at work and here is where, quite frankly, the pastor can trade in on the mystique that surrounds his office. *He* must make the approach. He must call, contact, write—whatever. People still hesitate to refuse Father. Besides, they are rightfully flattered at this implied confidence in them. In short, the pastor must spend much time in one of his chief tasks: identifying and enabling others to minister. It is he who most often will introduce the good but inactive parishioner into ministry. It is he who must ask for help on behalf of the community. No other person will do quite as well in this role. But why not? This is his charism, the charism of leadership. This, in turn, presupposes that he knows his people and has much contact with them, beyond a distant Sunday morning Mass time. As I described it in *The Christian Parish,* among our many contacts with people, two are our favorite: The Neighborhood Visitation every three weeks and our Saturday night dinners. Every Saturday night except during the summer, I cook dinner for a couple or individuals of the parish. Over the course of the years, not to mention over food and drinks, we can really get to know our people. It's a gospel occasion for the real recognition of one another in the breaking of the bread.

—2—

It happened quite by accident. One day a woman of the parish came up to me after Mass and said, "Father, thank God I'm all right now, and I appreciated your help going through this mastectomy. It was rough. But if there are ever any other women in the parish going through the same thing, let me know. I'd be glad to talk to them." That's when it hit me. Of course! Why not? There are so many people with particular problems and deep hurts that I have never experienced. What powerful ministers of healing they would make! What good effect on a one-to-one basis they could have! It was then that I went privately to various people I knew who had gone through difficult times and had come through them because of their faith and love. I asked them if they would be willing to minister to others if called upon? Would they be willing to let their names and phone numbers be listed in our annual Parish Booklet? As more and more said yes, we began what is now called our "One-to-One Ministry." What follows is a brief introductory description as it appeared in our recent Parish Booklet:

"Bear one another's burdens," Saint Paul has told us. And there is no one who can bear another's burdens, troubles, problems, and hardships as someone who has been there before you. Therefore, in the spirit of deep Christian love and courage, the names listed below all have personal experience with the problems listed. They are willing, having worked through these things themselves, to share whatever wisdom, faith and experience they have with others in the same situation. Call them if you need help. They will respect your confidence. They are "wounded healers," ready to help and listen in the name of the Lord.

Following is the list of problems. Each was accompanied by the name of the contact person with his or her phone number: Adoption, Alcoholism, Family of the Alcoholic, Amputee, Aging Parents, Brain-damaged Child, Cancer, Cardiac Visitation, Chronic Illness, Child of Divorced Parents, Death of a Child, Depression, Divorced and Remarried, Heart Attack, Hypoglycemia, Homosexuality, Loss of Job, Mastectomy, Sugar, Helping the Handicapped, and Terminal Illness.

The names we listed in our booklet were the real people of our community with a whole list of real, everyday problems. They are truly the "wounded healers" engaged in a ministry of healing. I might add that training and background are necessary here as well. There has to be not only a willingness to share from the heart but also practical resources and directives to share from the head.

Another example. I guess it was the experience of reading Jessica Mitford's book, *The American Way of Death,* years ago that put into focus what I and many others had been thinking for a long time: that funerals, like so much else in North America, had become another conspicuous consumer item; that much of the faith motif had literally and figuratively been buried; that we were on the way, and had long ago arrived at, the concept of funeral as gilded unreality, guilt trip and status symbol. Something of faith, belief in the resurrected Lord, was being lost in all this.

So I sought out a local undertaker, a man of faith himself, and expressed my concerns. He agreed that things had gone too far. He admitted that so often the size and cost of the funeral was in direct proportion to the guilt involved on the part of the survivors; that at times a circus atmosphere prevailed; that there was little understanding of the Christian symbols of hope; and that fanfare, music, limousine, and clock-flower arrangements quite smothered the realities of cross and resurrection. He encouraged me when I suggested that we might do away with long, multi-days wakes in the funeral parlor and reduce the wake to one night—and in the parish church! He went along with the use of regular cars instead of limousines, a simple wooden coffin that could be obtained for less than $300, the discouragement of too many flowers, and the encouragement of donations to needy causes. He was agreeable that, after the one-night wake service in church, we would have the Mass of Christian Burial at the next morning's regular community Mass.

So, I got busy, wrote up these proposals in a letter, stressed the faith element of a truly Christian burial, and sent this out to all of our parishioners. The response was very favorable among the people. I must say that it was considerably less so among the funeral industry. They began to write in their journals about this experiment. Three of their representatives politely came to see me, trying to talk some sense into me. One of them clearly indicated that if I persisted in this new approach, no one would bury me when I died. I replied that when I died it wasn't my problem. Besides, I had great confidence in the Board of Health and knew that sooner or later they would take action if no one else would.

Then they proposed all kinds of difficulties. What if the body fell out of the coffin? Are you covered by insurance? They suggested a whole series of possible disasters requiring second thoughts. They saved the ultimate argument for last: What if, in the attached-church-hall, on the very night of the wake in church, you had bingo! They could picture the anguished dilemma of a pastor forced to choose between Christian burial and bingo, knowing full well where his decision would fall. All kinds of flippant answers went through my mind, but I didn't need them since we do not have bingo. Eventually it all worked out. We do have wakes in the church for those who wish it (and most do). Our church is attached to a hall where there are bathrooms, kitchen facilities, and seating. The point of all this, however, is not so much the concept of church wakes, as it is the concept of ministry.

To meet this new need, we began our Lazarus Ministry. As the name suggests, the people on this committee, all of whom have known death, have various duties. They meet and welcome the body with the usual liturgical prayers when it is brought to church. They provide hospitality, coffee, cake, directions, presence, and they celebrate the evening wake service. They visit the family, help prepare the liturgy, and are there at the next's morning's community Mass. Their presence provides tone, practical direction by way of body language indicating when to sit or stand for those visitors and often parishioners who are not familiar with the Catholic Mass of Christian burial.

For the members of the Lazarus Ministry, training has been given. I gave them a course modeled after Msgr. Joseph Champlin's fine cassette program *Together By Your Side* (Ave Maria Press, Notre Dame, Ind.) which deals with how to comfort the sick, bereaved, and the dying. We had hospice people in from the local hospital. We gave them reading material and flyers. We showed them how to follow up and speak to the bereaved after the funeral is over and everybody has gone home. This is a ministry that comes straight from the community's experience and needs. Already, people do not mind that "Father" does not do the wake service. They are beginning to realize that these lay ministers are not substituting for Father's busyness or indifference, but are doing a ministerial task by baptismal right and personal charism. The Lazarus Ministry, therefore, is not a subdivision of mine, but a genuine home-grown gift which, in my capacity as pastor, I have identified and called forth.

Most dioceses today have some kind of Pre-Cana programs for engaged couples. These are now run almost exclusively by married couples with the priest doing a "guest spot." Years ago, it was almost totally the other way around. We have expanded on this in our own six-part (sometimes seven-part) marriage preparation program. (1) The engaged couple meets initially with the priest or deacon. (2) A sponsor couple is assigned who will be mentors, guides, supports, and examples of Christian marriage. The hope is that not only dialogue will take place but a sustaining friendship as well. (3) A session with our deacon-counsellor is arranged. (4) Pre-Cana conferences (given by our couples) or the engaged encounter weekend takes place. (5) A whole series of charming and delightful flyers are mailed to the boy and the girl separately that serve as discussion ice-breakers in their dates together. (6) There is a final meeting with the priest or deacon to firm up last-minute details or have further discussions. (7) Whenever we can, we have the couples, now married, back after a year to talk, exchange experiences, and give them more encouragement and help if warranted.

The point is not that these steps guarantee happy and stable marriages—we have our distressing and upsetting share of break-ups like everyone else—but that so many laypeople are so totally engaged in this ministry on so many levels.

One more brief example of ministry on the practical parish level. There is a national organization known as Contact. It is a Christian telephone hotline ministry. We have opened this up and sponsored this in the parish. It is entirely lay run and the people have to undergo a very intensive training period with frequent meetings and follow-ups afterward. They learn how to handle suicide, depression, and distress calls, and from all segments of society. They operate 24 hours a day in four-hour shifts. Truly this is dedication, a real reaching out and caring ministry. See other examples of ministries in the appendix.

Perhaps a practical instance of shared and responsible ministry can be cited in this example. Recently, for the first time since I can remember, a visiting priest failed to show up for a scheduled Sunday Mass. I was away celebrating Mass at a campsite for our family education group and the other priest who helps out was not at home. There were some 400 people in church waiting for Mass—and no priest. There were concern and anxiety, but not panic. Some of the people simply took charge and conducted a paraliturgy. They introduced the opening hymn, read the scriptures, gave a short talk, distributed communion, and led the closing hymn. They were able to do this because years ago I had introduced the chanting of the Divine Office (one of the hours or sections) on every Wednesday of the week in place of daily Mass. The point was to train the people in other forms of official worship besides the Mass. Because of such exposure, the people were able to take charge in the "missing priest emergency" rather than have the people aimlessly just trickle home. An attitude of baptismal confidence and competency made this possible.

There are two final things that need mentioning as we seek to translate shared ministry on the parish level. The first harkens back to Peter Rudge's remark that the way a parish organizes its common life tells more about its real priorities than all the sermons it preaches and mission statements it makes. One of these very practical organized priorities is money. Where a parish allots its (limited) money says a great deal about its philosophy and its vision. For the systemic parish, some money must always be earmarked for the development of the laity's ministry.

There are three instances in our parish that I can share here. When we first discussed our permanent married deacons role years ago, it was decided that, given his own temperament, and the parish's needs, we would send him away to Iona University to get his degree in counselling. This meant a hardship for him, for this was a long course. It was a hardship for us, for it meant not having him around too much for three years, not to mention paying his way, tuition, and books. But we did, and in turn we have a qualified deacon who gives several nights a week to counselling in the parish. Fordham University, through the courtesy of Gloria Durka, offered us a full time scholarship for someone from the parish, someone who would return to minister to the parish in Family Ministry. We gladly accepted, interviewed people and we sent a woman precisely for this purpose. She returned to give freely of her time and talent to us. The third instance of our interest in formation of lay ministers came from an opportunity from the Trinity Counselling Service in Princeton, N.J. They had a number of limited spaces for a two-year course in Family Counselling. The tuition was $1,200 a year. The parish agreed to send a man who could get off from his work once a week and who, in turn, gives freely of his expertise to the parish now that the course is finished. The point is that such prioritizing of money tells the people about our posture of shared ministry, our seriousness about collaboration.

The second thing that needs to be mentioned is the hope that the threefold building blocks are apparent behind all these movements. You recall that we cited three such building blocks: community, servant-leadership, and formation. The examples we have given are community projects with the knowledge and consent of the community and for the community's spiritual and physical needs. The ministers arise from community. They are homegrown products from all walks of life. They all receive some kind of training in their specific ministries and are offered many opportunities for continued spiritual formation and depth so that they may indeed realize that they are servants.

—3—

As a parish we still have far to go. As a parish, we know that other parishes labor under different circumstances, deal with special ethnic groups or inner-city poverty or many variations of neighborhoods and peoples. We try to learn from the heroes and heroines who minister in these places.[1] By the same token, we are where we are and must do our best and keep ourselves under judgment. We know we still have far to go. We know that our sensitivities aren't always what they should be. We know that a more thorough and overt dedication to social justice is needed. And there are our failures, shortcomings, blind spots, and daily betrayals to reckon with. But we're not talking about these things for which we must repent. We are talking about shared and collaborative ministry. We are talking about striving, however imperfectly, for the ideal of the systemic parish where we try to work together and foster interdependency. We're talking about many of the traditions from the first section of this book applied to our present circumstances. We're hoping that we're on our way to becoming Real.

The processes of enablement, empowerment, and encouragement are not easy. In fact, they are much harder. It was easier in the old days to bark out orders on Sunday morning and retire to the counting room. This "new" way is so damned imperfect, so vulnerable and, often, so untidy. But then we pick up the New Testament and there they are: all the very same nonsense, idolatry, favoritism, rivalries. But there, too, is the risen Jesus in their midst calling, healing, reconciling, and making his word powerful and fruitful in spite of all. There too is the many-gifted community, struggling for direction, sharing ministries, and striving for that ideal that Luke, in his comfortable hindsight, inflates as one of devotion "to the apostles' teaching, and fellowship, to the breaking of the bread and the prayers ... and they sold their possessions and goods and distributed them to all, as any had need" (Acts 2:42ff). Maybe it was those "varieties of gifts ... and varieties of service" (1 Cor 12:4) that somehow made it all work out.

In any case, in our own anxious times, we are backing off from an over-centralized and too top heavy church and taking a second look at these "varieties" of local community gifts and services. It is possible that we may do much worse than the first generations of Christians who took this path. Then, again, we may do much better. The roots are there. The Spirit is here.

Epilogue

At the end of his novel, *The Clowns of God,* a story of the imminent end of the world through nuclear bombardment, Morris West offers an old and attractive solution for the survival of humanity and the church. Under the guidance of the mysterious Christ figure, Mr. Atha, remnants of people are gathered into small communal groups in the hidden recesses of the mountains all over the world. The group in this book is a motley crew of people, from the former pope, Gregory XVIII, to the cynical psychology professor, to a young idealist. Mr. Atha speaks to them inside the mountain:

> ...First, you should know that you are not here by your own design. You were led here, step by step, on different roads, through many apparent accidents, but, always, it was the finger of God that beckoned you. You are not the only community thus brought together. There are many others all over the world: in the forests of Russia, in the jungles of Brazil, in places you would never dream. They are all different; because men's needs and habits are different. Yet, they are all the same, because they have followed the same beckoning finger, and bonded themselves by the same love. They did not do this of themselves. They could not, just as you could not, without a special prompting of grace. You were prompted for a reason. Even as I speak, the adversary begins to stalk the earth, roaring destruction! So, in the evil times which are now upon us, you are chosen to keep the small flame of love alight, to nurture the seeds of goodness in this small place, until the day when the Spirit sends you out to light other candles in a dark land and plant new seeds in a blackened earth.[1]

The novel and the solution gain credibility in a world such as ours today. Consider:

- A recent Associated Press release states: "The world rate of military spending is running about $1 million a minute, the Stockholm International Peace Research Institute said today in its 12th annual report."

- The press easily speaks of the "Nuclear Club" with six countries already possessing built-and-tested nuclear devices, nine more countries with the ready capacity to do so, twelve more who can and will have the bomb in six years and four more countries who will join them in seven to ten more years. Within a decade then, thirty-one countries will have nature's most terrible force in their hands. A force that was said to be safe only in the hands of God. In frail, jealous, or angry hands all must be considered lost. The late C.P. Snow was right in warning us some twenty years ago that "we know, with the certainty of established truth, that if enough of these weapons are made by enough different states, some of them are going to blow up—through accident, folly or madness."

Monies spent on military hardware and so diverted from peaceful uses is the subject of this report: Seven percent of the military outlays from fiscal 1981 to 1986 equals $100 billion, which in turn is the cost of rehabilitating the United States steel industry so that it is again the most efficient in the world.... The cost overrun, to 1981, on the Navy's Aeris-Cruiser program is $8.4 billion which in turn is comprehensive research-and-development effort needed to produce 80 to 100 mile per gallon cars.... Two B-1 Bombers equals $400 million, which in turn is the cost of rebuilding Cleveland's water supply system. The cost of unjustified non-combat Pentagon aircraft equals $6.8 billion which in turn equals six years of capital investment that is needed to rehabilitate New York City transit.... The cost overrun, to 1981, on the Army's heavy tank (MK-1) program equals $13 billion which in turn equals the shortfall of capital needed for maintaining water supplies of 150 United States cities for the next 20 years.... One nuclear (SSN-688) attack submarine equals $582 million which in turn equals the cost of 100 miles of electrified rail right-of-way.[2] These mind-boggling costs are incredible enough when deflected from industry and production, but what about when deflected from the mouths of the world's starving? Such astronomical figures underline more than ever the 1976 Vatican statement to the United Nations condemning "unreservedly" the arms race as an "act of aggression, which amounts to a crime, for ... by their cost alone, armaments kill the poor by causing them to starve."

An August 6, 1981 news item tells of an updated "white paper" on the 36th anniversary of the dropping of the atom bomb on Hiroshima. It says that "in almost every area of life the long-term consequences were more serious than earlier studies" indicated. Such consequences range from irreversible injuries to cells, tissues, and organs to the eye damage called "atomic bomb cataracts" to the "emotionally and intellectually retarded" children who were babies in the womb when the bomb was dropped, to, above all, the "psychological and spiritual shock" to all. As the study said, the magnitude of the atomic destruction "cannot be dismissed as just another hazard of war." It is better termed "genocide—for it is a complete negation of human existence." And the nuclear arms race goes on.

Other items are too numerous and too familiar to mention: water pollution, pesticides, toxic wastes. Destruction hangs over us like a smog giving rise to all kinds of fundamentalists who by their tapes, television sermons and books are scaring the hell out of people hoping to usher them into their guaranteed and elitist fold in time for the "rapture." Not to mention the growing groups of "survivalists" who hoard their dried foods on beneath-the-earth shelves and their cache of guns to fight off hungry neighbors and oved ones. Signs of the apocalyptic times are the 240 underground ondominiums built in Laverkin, Utah by Survive Tomorrow, Inc.

—2—

There are other dangers to grate on our moral, physical and piritual lives. Figures from the National Center for Health Studies how that by 1979 there were four and a half percent more divorces than the preceding year and triple the number reported 20 years earlier. Almost 1.2 million children joined the ranks of youngsters under 18 who have divorced parents. Another headline in the papers tells it all: "Teenagers Call Illicit Drugs: One of Life's Commonplaces." Abortions are at an all-time record high, especially among teenage girls, and teenage girls account for 11 percent of the nation's live births. To mention the alarming cases of child abuse, crime in the streets and white collar crime is only to recite some of the sorrows we have learned to live with.

The same disarray is in our church. We face large defections from the mainline organized religions and most surveys keep confirming the mass exodus of the young. They are not hostile, just indifferent. They say, "The church doesn't say anything to me," and they are often right. It's not just Vatican II fallout. It's the uncertainity of what it means to be religious, to be Catholic. They find a disconcerting lack of spirituality in the church, yet, they are hungering for it for they flock consistently to the latest messiahs elsewhere. They know not their spiritual roots, their mystics, their exquisite traditions of prayer. The young of today are almost total religious illiterates as every survey shows. Their consciences have been so desensitized that one can hardly say that they are morally responsible. Their morality is formed by the media, their heroes are basically nihilists, the moral perceptions of reality colored by the fantasies of television, yet, because they are human, they remain seekers, remain susceptible to divine surprises.

The older generation suffers and suffers terribly when their children do not and cannot drink deep from their religious, cultural and moral heritage which means so much to them and for which their parents and grandparents died. They stand back aghast at the lack of common non-negotiable values that bind: the unspoken, taken-for-granted priorities that cement relationships, interpret life and unite people in time of crisis. There's a beautiful passage from the pen of that marvelous writer, Willa Cather, in her book *Obscure Destinies*. In the story entitled "Neighbor Rosicky," Rosicky has just returned from the doctor, and his wife Mary is looking at him, anxious about the report and how much truth he is telling her.

Mary sat watching him intently, trying to find any change in his face. It is hard to see anyone who has become like your own body to you... He was fifteen years older than Mary, but she had hardly ever thought about it before. He was her man, and the kind of man she liked. She was rough, and he was gentle—city-bred, as she always said. They had been shipmates on a rough voyage and had stood by each other in trying times. Life had gone well with them because, at the bottom, they had the same ideas about life. They agreed, without discussion, as to what was most important and what was secondary. They didn't often exchange opinions, even in Czech—it was as if they had the same thought together. A good deal had to be sacrificed and thrown overboard in a hard life like theirs, and they had never disagreed as to the things that could go....[3]

Such are the shared heritage and experiences that make it all worthwhile. But for many such a foundational tradition does not exist. There *are* no enduring values, no unexamined assumptions. Everything is in flux, relative, negotiable. The only way to live is to "hang loose" and keep one's options open. Commitments are for as long as you can stand them. Can anyone say yes forever? In the eyes of many, neighbor Rosicky and his wife Mary are quaint, square, unliberated.

Parents are hurt when their children reject their values. They face all kinds of horrid dilemmas. Shall we attend our son's wedding outside the church to a divorced woman? How do we introduce our daughter's live-in boyfriend? We're against abortion, but our high schooler just can't drop out to raise a baby. Are we imposing our middle class values on them, as they say? What is it they are dumping on us? Is there any family in town, even the best, that does not know some kind of kinky sorrow as neopaganism and a debilitated Christianity clash? Liberal priests and nuns who tossed out sin with the Friday abstinence, and inadequate and uninformed religion teachers—these, our former mainstays, helpers, and supports, have betrayed us. So the feelings run.

Someone asked me what I, as a parish priest, thought were the two things people needed most desperately today. I answered without hesitation: hope and a sense of meaning. People want some assurance that things will settle down, that family life, relationships, nuclear threat will all somehow work themselves out. They need a sense that there are brighter days ahead and that, meanwhile, God is with them and that in his Christ, he will make all things new again. They need a sense of meaning, because more and more they feel deep in their bones a sense of powerlessness. Each day they are made aware that big government, big business control their lives and the lives of most of the world's population. Corporate decisions affect a majority of the people without their knowledge or consent.

People feel out of control in the areas closest to them and their values. They express it by saying that *they* don't make the pornographic movies; they have no control over what is on television; they don't publish the lurid books in public places that entice their adolescents; they didn't invent the flashy non-nutritional products their kids eat; they don't produce violent television shows; they are not happy with inferior educational standards and teachers who can't spell; they deplore shoddy workmanship and slipshod services. They do not write or distribute such me-orientated books such as *Be Your Own Best Friend* or *How to Live Alone and Like It.* They are suspicious of the constant shallow stream of educational, religious, and social fads. They are inundated by these and a thousand other "slings and arrows of outrageous fortune," as Shakespeare phrases it, and they feel powerless against them all. They need hope, they need a sense of meaning, they need something to keep themselves from being changed. They scream in frustration.

Elie Wiesel tells the story about a faithful Jew, a just man who came to a sinful town, determined to save the people from destruction. Night and day he walked the streets preaching against greed and theft and falsehood and indifference. At the beginning the people listened and smiled condescendingly. Then they stopped listening; he no longer even amused them. The killers went on killing and the wise kept silent as if there were no just man in their midst. One day a child, puzzled by the unfortunate preacher and feeling sorry for him, asked, "Poor stranger, you shout and you wear yourself out. Don't you see that it's hopeless"? "Yes, I see," answered the just man. "Then why do you go on?" "I'll tell you why. I am not sure to what extent, if any, *I* can change these people, but if I still shout today and if I still scream, it is to prevent them from changing *me.*" Many are screaming, screaming for hope, for meaning.

The clergy feel it too. I talk to them, particularly to the young ones. They all tell me the same story, the same two basic complaints. They do not sense any direction, any vision in the church they serve; there are no visionary and imaginative leaders, just episcopal and clerical politicians doing business as usual. The enterprise called the church doesn't seem to be going anywhere; the priorities seem to be off center, at least far enough away from the gospel. Then comes the second lament: there is such a lack of support. "No one up there (chancery) cares whether I live or die, what I'm doing, how or why." There's no fraternity, no caring, no affirmation. All work is personal to the extent that when the man goes, his work often goes as well. There is no over-all plan, direction, inspiration, vision. Is this why they leave? Is this why they do not come?

—3—

Surely this is a sad litany of troubles, hardly designed to cheer us up. So, then, where does this little sermon, disguised as an epilogue, leave us? What does it tell us about ministry? I think it tells us more about attitudes in ministry than anything else. Maybe for some, Mr. Atha's warning that evil times are upon us and we must keep the small flame of love alight means that literally we should start all over again. Maybe we should make a career out of "Small Is Beautiful" and rebuild our parishes, communities, and monasteries with a handful of dedicated people. Maybe we should dismantle our large, corporate parish structures. Maybe we should decentralize our chanceries and multiply our dioceses and bishops a thousandfold so we can get to know one another. As Sandra Schneiders says:

> Where is faith ... most alive and effective? It seems to be in small grassroots communities, charismatic groups, small local groups of religious men or women, life-revision groups, feminist support groups, alternative worshipping communities, service groups ... and prayer groups of all kinds. What faith seems to be for these people is a kind of hermeneutic, that is, a kind of interpretation which they apply to their everyday experience and then use for personal and social transformation."[4]

Maybe this is the way we should be going. I don't know. Anyway, I speak more of an attitude in ministry that our reflections should influence.

This means that as we contemplate the radical ramifications of shared and collaborative ministry we must do so in our world context, that is, not with a sense of jockeying for power and authority, but with a genuine sense of common mission. We are today's pioneers. Our ministry is fundamentally one of evangelization in a pagan world. We cannot afford the luxury of infighting. We're starting from scratch for we can no longer assume either Christian principles or Christian culture. Therefore our lifestyle will say as much as our words. Our ministerial lives must be different. Mere professional competence will no longer do. The times are urgent. It is our changed lives that will compel others to listen to us. The call to genuine holiness is the minister's call.

I sometimes worry that the approach to our current crises in the church is so exclusively secular. We often seem to be like a board of directors of a large company. We say, "We're losing customers. What can we do to win them back? How can we keep them from choosing other brands?" I get the feeling that many of our bishops see the whole issue of ministry solely from the political point of view. "Well," they say, "we've got this terrible problem, you see. There's so few priests and little prospect of any significant numbers on the horizon. So let's pull in the laity and parcel out some of the clerical jobs."

There is a distinct impression at times that if by some miracle we were inundated by more than enough priests, the whole issue of lay ministry would be dropped. And the laity too sometimes see ministry as a chance to get in on the ecclesiastical act, a chance for status in the system so long denied to them. Not that many bishops or laity seem to challenge the system itself; they do not seem to acknowledge a whole new context in which Christianity must struggle. For, if anything, ministry should be seen as a code word for the mixture of the ordained and non-ordained in a fundamentally new start of a people bonded together to reintroduce the Good News to the world. Ministers should take on the mind-set of modern missionaries who no longer move into a new land anxious to proselytize and add numbers to the worldwide Catholic Directory as their first priority. Rather, the modern missionaries, clergy and lay, go first and live the gospel. They bear witness. They compete by the purity of their lives and the evidence of their charity and so in time—maybe decades—make others see another way. And even then, there is a long catechumenate in deference to a real conversion from paganism.

This is why, you see, the reflections on history, theology, and practical questions we made in this book are not intended to provide ammunition for one side or another. They are meant to provide common ground for both clergy and laity on which to build anew. What has been written is not intended merely to hasten us into new programs. We will not survive standing around, only composing new strategies. We will survive only on our knees. A book on ministry, however dispassionately written (well, almost) for the sake of exposition, does not absolve us from deep reflection on the gospel. It does not release us from the necessity of the desert experience or the wisdom of the fathers. We are so programmed to punch a computer key board for answers that we become impatient with what is needed most: time to be open to the Spirit. Our pursuit of ministry, limited to the head, at times distracts us from asking the essential question, and finding the essential answer in the heart: "To whom shall we go: you have the words of eternal life."

There's a story about one of the desert fathers, named Arsenius. It seems that some monks from Alexandria were going near the dwelling of this famous and holy man. In fact, they were going to a town called Thebaid to look for some flax. They said to one another, "While we're in the area, let's drop by and see Abba Arsenius." They did, and the monk at the door took their message and went to Abba Arsenius and said, "Some of the brothers from Alexandria wish to see you." Arsenius answered, "Ask them why they have come." Having learned that they were here mainly to look for flax, the monk reported this to Abba Arsenius who said, "They will certainly not see my face, for they have not come on my account, but because of their own work. Make them rest and send them away in peace and tell them the old man cannot receive them."[5] This may sound harsh to our ears but the point is a gospel one: let the dead bury their dead and come follow me. No man can serve two masters. Which means that when we're really serious about seeking the person of Jesus and not only our ministerial expertise and degrees, then we shall see his face.

Again, all of our doomsdaying remarks of the preceding pages are designed to force us to real hope, one based on Jesus. Yes, things are becoming "unglued" as Marc Connolly's angel said. Yes, we are drowning, but we must let people know through our ministry that there is someone walking on the water to save us. Yes, we are in danger of nuclear annihilation. people do speak seriously about megaton killings. Resources are finite after all, and mere cleverness alone will not respond to these cosmic issues. Holiness will respond, and frequently it will be the holiness rooted in the absurdity of the cross. Have we forgotten that, after all, things were pretty bleak two thousand years ago? The original Christian minister started out small with twelve people. He spent a large share of his ministry in prayer. He wasn't terribly effective and, in fact, wound up as a classic failure. But to this day he ministers to us. Still, if no disciple is above his master, then we ministers surely must adopt the same priorities. That's all this epilogue really wants to say.

Notes

Chapter One

1. Walter J. Burghardt, "What Is a Priest?" *The Way,* Supplement, No. 23 (Autumn 1974)., p. 56.
2. John A. Coleman, "The Future of Ministry," *America,* (March 28, 1981).
3. Eugene H. Maly, "The Priest and Sacred Scripture," (Washington, D.C.: United States Catholic Conference, 1971), p. 4.
4. The style of church rule called Presbyterianism comes from this.
5. We must remember that such names as Paul and Barnabas and a few other names we have come from Luke. He, however, is telling us about one small group of evangelists. There must have been scores of others unknown to us to spread Christianity so rapidly and to so many places.
6. Hans Kung feels that there was a leaderless community at Corinth with the implication that there was no "priest" to celebrate the eucharist. Rather it was celebrated by non-ordained baptized persons. As might be expected, the Congregation for the Doctrine and Faith disputes this and in turn Kung defends his position. See *The Kung Dialogue* (Washington, D.C.: 1980), pp. 45-47.
7. Eugene H. Maly, Op. Cit. p. 28. See also Raymond E. Brown's *Priest and Bishop: Biblical Reflections* (New York: Paulist Press, 1970), p. 13 ff.

Chapter Two

1. Hans Lietzmann, *The Founding of the Church Universal* (Meridian, 1963), pp. 54-61.
2. See Bernard Botte, "Christian People and Hierarchy in the Apostolic Tradition of St. Hippolytus," in *Roles in the Liturgical Assembly* (New York: Pueblo Publishing Co., 1981), p. 62.
3. See Joseph H. Crehan, S.J., "Priesthood, Kingship, and Prophecy," in *Theological Studies,* Vol. 42, No. 2 (June 1981), pp. 216 ff.
4. Bernard Cooke, *Ministry to Word and Sacraments* (Philadelphia: Fortress Press, 1976), pp. 528-529.
5. Herve-Marie Legrand, "The Presidency of the Eucharist According to the Ancient Tradition," *Worship,* Vol. 53, No. 5 (September 1979), p. 427.
6. ibid. p. 430.
7. See Jaroslav Pelikan, *The Emergence of the Catholic Tradition* (Chicago: University of Chicago Press, 1971), pp. 1-27. Also see Daniel J. Harrington S.J., *God's People in Christ,* (Philadelphia: Fortress Press, 1980). We should also note that Judaism's having "had its day" must be reviewed in the light of the fact that it is still here. The relationship between this fact, Christianity and God's will, is a vexing one.
8. Bernard Cooke, op. cit. p. 43.
9. Quoted in the article "Institutionalized Religion" in T. Patrick Burke, *The Word in History,* Sheed & Ward, 1966. I am indebted for the preceding pages to John T. Pawlikowski's fine article, "The Minister As Pharisee" in *Commonweal,* January 21, 1972, pages 369 ff.

10. Joseph H. Crehan, S.J., op. cit. p. 216 ff.
11. James A. Mohler, S.J. *The Origin and Evolution of the Preisthood,* (New York: Alba House,) pages 105, 106. See also William J. Bausch, *A New Look at the Sacraments* (Mystic, Ct.: Twenty-Third Publications, 1977) and Joseph Martos, *Doors to the Sacred,* (Garden City, N.Y.: Doubleday) 1981.

Chapter Three

1. This tension will dramatically come to a head in the French Revolution when the lower clergy will emerge as potent factors in the overthrow of the aristocratic higher clergy.
2. Quoted by James A. Mohler, S.J., op. cit. p. 83.
3. Maria Harris, *Portrait of Youth Ministry* (Ramsey, N.J.: Paulist Press, 1981), p. 13. I am indebted to her for the development of this paragraph.
4. George W. MacRae, *The Living Light,* Vol. 14, No. 2 (Summer 1977), p. 173.
5. See William J. Bausch, *A New Look at the Sacraments.*
6. Epistles, 25.8, 11 PL 20, 561.
7. Ross Mackenzie, "The Eucharist as Sacrifice," *Journal of Ecumenical Studies,* Vol. 15, No. 3 (Summer 1978), p. 426. This whole exchange between two theologians, one Catholic and the other Reform, is worth reading.
8. ibid. p. 435.
9. Raymond E. Brown, "Three Biblical Concepts of Priesthood," *Catholic Mind,* Vol. 58, No. 1341 (March 1980), p. 18.
10. Eugene Maly, op. cit. p. 12.
11. Walter J. Burghardt, op. cit. pp. 61, 62.
12. William R. Burrows, *New Ministries: The Global Context* (Maryknoll, N.Y.: Orbis Books 1980), p. 61.
13. Raymond E. Brown, op. cit. p. 16.
14. CE, 10
15. Perhaps this deserves more than a footnote, but it should be recorded here that Vatican II's insistence that there is a genuine and intrinsic difference "in kind and not just in degree" (*Lumen Gentium,* 2, No., 10)—reflecting the Council of Trent's strong affirmation (D. 957, 961, 2300)—between the ordained priesthood and the priesthood of all believers is hard to analyze. Somehow the one implies a defect in the other and it is not clear just what that is. If, as we have seen, it may be possible in an emergency for a Christian to celebrate any and all of the sacraments, including the eucharist, and to preside over the community, then that "essential" difference is elusive and difficult to locate. See "The Ordained Ministerial Presbyterate: A Position Paper" by D. Aschbeck in *Schola* 1, (1978), pp. 61 ff.
16. Hans Kung, *The Church* (New York: Sheed and Ward 1967), p. 439.
17. Raymond E. Brown, op. cit. p. 20.
18. Eric W. Gritsch and Robert W. Jenson, *Lutheranism* (Philadelphia: Fortress Press, 1976), p. 122.

Chapter Four

1. Morris West, *The Clowns of God* (New York: William Morrow and Co. Inc., 1981), p. 66.

2. ibid. p. 44.
3. Abigail McCarthy, "Creativity and Community: The Lay Responsibility" in *At the Edge of Hope* (New York: Seabury Press, 1978), p. 86.
4. "Called and Gifted: Catholic Laity," November 1-13, 1980.
5. Daniel Yankelovich, *New Rules in American Life: Searching for Self-Fulfillment in a World Turned Upside Down.* Excerpted in *Psychology Today,* (April 1981), p. 44.
6. ibid, p. 78.
7. ibid, p. 85.
8. John Heigl, "Basic Communities in Tanzania," *America,* (April 11, 1981), p. 299.
9. ibid.
10. Gottfried Deelan, "The Church On Its Way to the People: Basic Christian Communities in Brazil." *Cross Currents,* Vol. 30, No. 4 (Winter 1980-1981), p. 390. Outline is slightly adapted.
11. ibid. p. 391.
12. National Bulletin on Liturgy, (May-June, 1981), Vol. 14, No. 79 Ottawa, Ontario.

Chapter Five

1. Cyrille Vogel, "Is Presbyteral Ordination of the Celebrant a Condition for the Celebration of the Eucharist?" in *Roles in the Liturgical Assembly* (New York: Pueblo Publishing Co., 1981), p. 340. footnote 27.
2. Edward Schillebeeckx, *Ministry* (New York: Crossroad, 1981), p. 13. For examples of communities that do have a eucharistic celebration without authorization, especially those by women, see *National Catholic Reporter,* Vol. 17, No. 35 (July 17, 1981).
3. Cyrille Vogel, op. cit. p. 263.
4. See "The Eucharist Today" in *Theology Digest,* Vol. 25, No. 1 (Spring 1977), especially pp. 30 and 31.
5. Edward Schillebeeckx, "Catholic Understanding of Office" in *Theological Studies,* Vol. 30, No. 4 (December 1969), p. 569.
6. For example, this is the recommendation of Gabriel March in *Pro Mundi Vita Bulletin,* (July 1980).
7. Jurgen Moltmann, "The Diaconal Church in the Context of the Kingdom of God" in *Hope for the Church* (Nashville: Abingdon, 1979), p. 21. See also Andrew Greeley, *et al, Parish, Priest and People* (Chicago: Thomas More Press, 1981).
8. Henri J. Nouwen, *Clowning in Rome* (Garden City, N.Y.: Image Books, 1979), pp. 48-49.
9. Archbishop Joseph Bernardin, "Reflections on the Ministerial Priesthood," *Origins,* (Vol. 11, No. 5 (June 18, 1981), p. 75.
10. Eugene H. Maly, op. cit. p. 15.
11. *Catholic Biblical Quarterly,* Vol. 41, No. 41 (October 1979). One of the best summaries of the issue of women's ordination is Paul K. Jewett's book, *The Ordination of Women* (Grand Rapids, Mich: Wm. Eerdmans Publishing Co., 1980). For a different view, see Jerome D. Quinn, "New Testament Data on Priestly Ordination," in *America,* (September 6, 1980), p. 94 ff.
12. See Marian Schwab's article, "Dancing Sarah's Circle" in *The Priest* (July-August,

1981) and also Michael Slusser's article "Women in the Process of Change: Our Ministry to Them and Their Ministries" in the same magazine, (May 1981).

13. John H. Westerhoff III and William H. Willimon, *Liturgy and Learning: Through the Life Cycle* (New York: Seabury Press, 1980), pp. 143, 144.
14. William K. McElvaney, *The People of God in Ministry* (Nashville: Abingdon, 1981), pp. 19, 20.
15. Walter Burghardt, op. cit. pp. 58, 59.
16. Avery Dulles, "Imaging the Church for the 1980's" in *Thought,* Fordham University Quarterly, Vol. LVI. No. 221 (June 1981).
17. Richard P. McBrien, *Catholicism,* Vol. II, (Minneapolis: Winston Press, 1980), p. 811.
18. David Ashbeck, op. cit. p. 68.
19. ibid.
20. See the model due process plan for the Diocese of Belleville, Illinois, *Origins,* Vol. II, No. 1 (May 21, 1981).
21. *The Catholic Review,* Baltimore, Maryland, (October 19, 1979).

Chapter Six

1. David N. Power, *Gifts That Differ: Lay Ministeries Established and Unestablished* (New York: Pueblo Publishing Co., 1981), p. 140.
2. Loughlan Sofield, S.T., "Tomorrow's Lay Ministry," in *Human Development* Vol. 1, No. 4 (Winter 1980), pp. 18 ff.
3. See Sue Elsesser in *Origins,* Vol. 10, No. 10 (August 14, 1980).
4. Virginia Sullivan Finn, "The Web of the World, Psychological and Sociological Aspects of Sharing Ministry Responsibility," in *Growing Together: Conference on Shared Ministry,* (Washington D.C.: National Council Catholic Bishops, 1980) pp. 40-42.

Chapter Seven

1. Daniel Yankelovich, op. cit. p. 40.
2. See William J. Bausch *The Christian Parish: Whispers of the Risen Christ,* (Mystic, Ct.: Twenty-Third Publications, 1980). Also, see Andrew Greeley, *et al, Parish, Priest and People,* (Chicago, Ill.: Thomas More Association, 1981).
3. Robert K. Greenleaf, *Servant Leadership* (Ramsey, N.J.: Paulist Press, 1977), p. 10. It is significant that the Bishops' Committee on "Priestly Life and Ministry" entitles its report *As One Who Serves* (Washington, D.C.: United States Catholic Conference, 1977).
4. John Gallen, *New Catholic World,* Vol. 224, No. 1342 (July-August, 1981), p. 149.
5. Henri J. Nouwen, "The Monk and the Cripple," in *Growing Together,* op. cit. pp. 6 and 7.
6. Alfred C. Hughes, *Preparing for Church Ministry* (Denville, N.J.: Dimension Books, 1979), p. 19.
7. From his autobiography, *Report to Greco,* as quoted in James C. Fenhagen's book,

More Than Wanders (New York: Seabury Press, 1978).

8. Theresa Monroe, *Growing Together,* op. cit. p. 64.

9. Quoted by William K. McElvaney, op. cit. p. 49.

Chapter Eight

1. George Gallup Jr. and David Poling, *The Search for America's Faith* (Nashville: Abingdon, 1980), p. 88. See also J. Russell Hale's, *The Unchurched* (New York: Harper & Row, 1980).

2. ibid. pp. 101-102.

3. ibid. p. 126.

4. Described in James C. Fenhagen's book, *Mutual Ministry* (New York: Seabury Press, 1977), pp. 101 ff.

5. Robert G. Howes, "Support Your Local Priest," in *The Priest,* (July-August, 1981), p. 16. See also Robert A. Graham, S.J., "A New Assault on the Priesthood" in *Columbia,* (April, 1981), p. 3 and, in a slightly different vein, Peter E. Fink's "The Other Side of the Priesthood" in *America,* (April 11, 1981), pp. 291 ff.

6. John H. Westerhoff III and William H. Willimon, op. cit., p. 143.

7. Henri J. Nouwen, in *Action Information* (Mount St. Alban, Washington D.C.: Alban Institute, Jan.-Feb. 1981).

8. Will D. Campbell, *Brother to a Dragonfly* (New York: Seabury Press, 1977), pp. 150-151.

Chapter Nine

1. See, for example, "Life in an Inner City Parish" by Father X in *Our Sunday Visitor,* (August 2, 1981), pp. 12 ff.

Epilogue

1. Morris West, op. cit. p. 363.

2. Seymour Melman, "Looting the Means of Production," *The New York Times,* (Sunday, July 26, 1981), p. E 21.

3. Willa Cather, *Obscure Destinies,* (Franklin Center, Pa.: The Franklin Library 1981), p. 165.

4. Sandra M. Schneiders, IHM, "The Ministry of the Word and Contemporary Catholic Education" in *Ministry and Education,* edited by Mary C. Boys, (Winona, Minn.: Saint Mary's Press, 1981), p. 24.

5. From Benedicta Ward, *The Desert Christian: Sayings of the Desert Fathers* (New York: Macmillan Co., 1971), p. 13.

Appendix
Parish Booklet

St. Mary's Parish, Colts Neck, N.J. (07722) publishes an annual resource booklet. It is mailed free to all parishioners; others can purchase for $1.50. In it is all necessary information about the parish: its organization, its people, its services. The booklet provides instant communication for the parish members and includes an annual calendar of events.

The following is a brief outline of the booklet's contents, as well as a few sample pages.

Page 1: Telephone numbers, Mass schedules, key names.
Page 2: Names and brief biographies of parish staff.
Page 3: Theme for the Year.
Pages 4-54: The seven key sections of the booklet.

Part I: Committees and Organizations

Listed here are the names of the members of the Parish Assembly, which includes the Parish Council and the Parish Committees such as: the Christian Stewardship Committee; the buildings and Grounds Committee; the Christian Gospel Concerns Committee (subdivided into the Samaritans, the Lazarus Confraternity, and the Crisis Room); the Spiritual Life Committee; the Liturgy Committee (subdivided into specific action groups such as Eucharistic Ministers, Lectors, Cantors and Organists, Folk Choir, Choir, Moppet Choir, Children's Choir, Singing Singles, Ushers, Altar Persons [male and female], Banners, Flowers, Church Maintenance, Altar Linens, Altar Bread).

Other specific groups include: Money Counters, Youth Ministry, Family Life Committee, Religious Education Committee, Bible School, Evangelization, Library, Christmas Decorating Group, Ministry of Hospitality, Groundkeepers.

Parish organizations that transcend specifics include: the Martha and Mary Guild, the Men's Parish Guild, the Holy Spirits, the Knights of Columbus, and the National Council of Catholic Women.

Part II: Religious Education

St. Mary's Parish offers a variety of programs, short courses, workshops, speakers, and events for adults, teens, the young, and preschoolers, as well as family education.

Part III: Liturgy and Spiritual Life

Both personal and communal opportunities are offered to deepen union with God. Sunday Mass schedules are included here, not only for St. Mary's but for surrounding parishes. Retreats, days of recollection, communal confessions, children's liturgies, and so on, are all scheduled throughout the year. The policies and practices for sacramental liturgies are explained in more detail.

Part IV: Parish Social Life

A calendar list of activities in this division includes: mini-breakfasts, parish picnics, balloons of hope, parish trips, dances, and women's bowling.

Part V: Special Affairs and Services

Information about leaders and programs include: Marriage Encounters; Pentecostal Groups; Cursillo; Professional Marriage, Family, and Individual Counselling; Drug Problem; Birthright; Exceptional Children; Alcoholism; Divorced and Separated Catholics; College Newsletter; Singles; Monmounth County H.O.P.E. (Helping Other People Evolve); Compassionate Friends; Pre-Cana; Parents and Friends Association; Monmounth-Ocean County Group on Learning Disability; Fellow Pilgrims; Ministry of One-to-One; St. Mary's Counselling Services.

Part VI: What's New This Year?

Because this section indicates the constant creativity that emerges from involved people in the parish, the following pages of the booklet are reproduced.

Part VII: Parish Calendar

The booklet's calendar pages are reproduced here to indicate the variety of services, opportunities, and activities in the parish.

The Parish Assembly meetings, to which all parishioners are invited are as follows (all Sunday afternoons): September 13, 1981, October 16, 1981, December 6, 1981, January 7, 1982, February 28, 1982 and May 16, 1982. The more you attend the meetings or speak to the Assembly members, the more your views are heard.

B. THE PARISH COMMITTEES

1. **The Christian Stewardship Committee** takes care of the parish books, keeps the financial records, reconciles the bank statements, prepares the annual diocesan financial report and advises the pastor on financial matters as well as provides him with an annual cost analysis of running the various buildings. Members are: Mike Smith, chairman (741-6643), Bill Dunn, Trudi Poole, Bill Huntley, Rudy Schellenberger, Martha Anne Cicero and Jim Desmond.

2. **The Buildings and Grounds Committee** oversees and advises about the material properties of the parish such as the need for repairs, preventative maintenance, fuel economy and future expension. Members of this committee are John Fee, chairman (842-3962), Joe Dobrowolski, John Laffey, Joe Henderson, Jr., Walt Hickson, Al Jakelis, Jack Mahoney, John Ruhnke, Tom Ryan, Ernest Schaflin, William Tibbitt and Walt Zimmerer. Their annual inspection and recommendation day is October 24, 1981.

3. **The Christian Gospel Concerns Committee.** In addition to the general parish social justice activities such as the monthly food collection, the annual cancer luncheon, the Senior Citizens' days of recollection, the children's envelope monies to Bread for the World and the one-to-one ministries, there are three organized areas under this committee.

a. The Samaritans. Members are Alex and Louise Basista, Judi Beitler, Corinne Bertrand, Dot Boese, Mary Rita Brennan, Sharon Burlew, Terry Cafiero, Tease Colando, Marie Curran, Linda Damen, Peggy De Pol, Simone Dietrich, Ellen Marie Dunn, Maureen Ferone, Jean Fitzgerald, Anita Gassert, Betty Guenther, William and Mildred Lanzaron, Rosemary Herold, Joanne Hiller, Maureen Knapp, Jean Lenz, Heidi Lohn, Walene Lutkewitte, Dee O'Malley, Jan Reddan, Linda Rossano, Stephen and Kathryn Schuster, May St. Germaine, Madeline Tibbitt, Mary Vanderbilt and Lorraine Walsh and Georganne Attardi who coordinates this group.

b. The Lazarus Confraternity. Members of this group are Tease Colando, Marie Curran, Walter Dowd, Jean Fitzgerald, Joan Henderson, Sarah Kuhlman, Rose Laccitiello, Russ Leahy, Marie Leeuw, Evelyn Mosher, Harold and Helen Owendoff, Madeline Tibbitt and Don Voss.

c. The Crisis Room. This refers to a group of people under the direction of Mike Morra (946-3953), who have undergone extensive training in handling emergency and stress telephone calls on our Crisis Room "hot line". In addition to handling such calls, they are training future volunteers.

4. The Spiritual Life Committee. Working with all parish organizations, this committee keeps abreast of the spiritual needs of the parish. It is working to develop a resource manual on available spiritual programs both at the parish and elsewhere. The committee is available for advice on continuing spiritual refreshment and growth for all parishioners. Members of this committee are Father Bausch, Sister Joan Koliss, Theresita Blake, Dot Boese, Eleanor Brady, Maryann Burke, Alfred Camarote, Lucille Castro, Tom Gassert, Lynn George, Thomas Hennessey, Sylvan and Walene Lutkewitte, John Marino, Carl Simone and Brother Robert Berger.

5. The Liturgy Committee advises, plans and assists in the parish liturgies. Members of this committee are Mary Rita Brennan (431-3451) and Harold Owendoff (747-0815) chairpersons, Elaine Baran, Dot Boese, Steve Carroll, Marie Curran, Peggy De Pol, Marie Dooley, Tom Gassert, Joan Henderson, Jean Lenz, Jack MacPhee, Ed and Una McCloud, Helen Owendoff, Mary Ring, Lou Schmitt, Joanna Taltavall, Madeline Tibbitt, Joan Vitale, Frank Wolff, Sister Joan Koliss and Father Bausch.

a. Eucharistic Ministers: Joseph Agnese, Dolores Bacsik, Dorothy Boese, Edward Chapman, John Conley, Sylvia DeVictoria, Maureen Kelly, Anton Kopp, Alice Roman, Gerri Tirpak.

b. The Lectors are Dot Boese, Marie Curran, Stan Drusdow, Mark Drusdow, Ray Flint, Florence Grant, Doris and Tom Hudak, Jean Knipper, John Laffey, Helen Owendoff, Peter Podesta, Janet Quackenbush, Robert Rauth, Jan Reddan, Margaret Ross, Barbara Schaflin, Carl Simone, Barbara Thomas, Madeline Tibbitt, Joseph Delmaster, Margery Gilbert and Joe Henderson, Jr.

c. The Cantors and Organists under Pat Picco (842-2073) are:
Cantors: Tom Baum Theresita Blake, Jack Brennan, Steve Carroll, Mary Carter, Dave Clarke, Pegge De Pol, Anne Henderson, Joan Henderson, Mary Howard, Jean Knipper, Russ Leahy, Jean Lenz, Mike Steinberger and George Towne.
Organists: Ray Bassford, Tease Colando, Bernie Coleman, Sister Rosemarie de Camilla, Joan Delmaster, Tom Gassert, Carla Gray, Joe Knipper, Regina Laffey, Jack MacPhee, Cindy Veselis, Alba Wagar, Jim Walthour and Barbara Zwolinski.

d. The Folk Choir under Steve Carroll (780-3454) are Elaine Baran, Linda Bingler, Mary Rita Brennan, Elaine Carroll, Jane Davis, Sue Desmond, Marie Dooley, Laura Gartland, Mary Fournier, Roseann Hazinski, Treasure Herman, Millie Illmensee, Carol Le Munyon, Marilynne, Morley, Jan Reddan, Nancy Runge, Maura Schmidt, Sister Therese Cahill and Rita Wagar. Guitarists are Ellie Christian, Sue Fiedler, Mary Howard, Eileen Malavet and Peter Wagar and Carl Baran plays the drums.

e. The Choir under Jack MacPhee (741-3852), director and Tom Gassert, organist, are Raymond Bassford Theresita Blake, Eleanor Brandy, Mary Carter, Ed Chapman, Dave Clarke, Joan Delmaster, Pegge De Pol, Agnes Duffy, Cecilia Fitzpatrick, Gary Flanagan, John Galligan, Anne Henderson, Joan Henderson, Joe Henderson, Jr., Therese and Tony Kopp, Russell Leady, Carol Le Munyon, Maureen Newall, Diana Piotrowski, Jan Reddan, Connie Reschke, Nancy Runge, Ann Scholtz, Bill Senn, Kathy and Michael Steinberger, George Towne, Joan Vitale, Jim Walthour and Bill Westbrook.

f. The Moppet Choir, under the direction of Joan Vitale (946-3840), are Christy Baker, Ann Castle, Barbara Daniele, Samantha De Cerce, Laura Donofries, Maryann Gallagher, Christine Luongo, Suzanne Marchner, Heather Murray, Cristen Newell, Vanessa Strnad, Heather Swenson, Elizabeth Thomas, Christine Greco, Amy Fitzpatrick, Jennifer Merwin and Lisa Vitale. Practice sessions are held on Thursday afternoons at 3:30 p.m.

g. The Children's Choir under the direction of Elaine Baran (774-3658) are: Lia Beard, Barrett Beard, Elissa Lynn Beard, Christine Beyer, Wendy Caliendo, Jennifer Johnston, Rosemary Le Munyon, Constance Oberle and Tasha Pomerleau. Practice is held on Tuesdays at 4:15 p.m.

h. The Singing Singles under Bernie Coleman (449-2637) are Donna Marie Irwin, Ted Myslinski, Janet Testaverde, Greg Tilling, Chris Zetlin and Bob Zetlin.

i. The Ushers under Frank Wolff (462-2066) are Robert Barklage, William Barrett, William Barth, John Beckley, Roger Boucher, Ralph Battista, Carol Casanova, Don Clark, Charles Camarata, Edward Connors, William Connors, Joseph Dobrowlski, Walter Dowd, Gerry Fitzgerald, Paul Fournier, John Ganley, George Illmensee, Jr., Frank Kubek, Albert Lohn, Sil Lukewitte, Joseph Nichols, Joseph O'Connor, William O'Malley, Harold Owendoff, James Pifer, Arthur Rodriquez, Al Ring, John Ruhnke, Edmund Toutounchi, Don Voss, Joseph Walsh and Steve Zwolinski.

j. The Altar Persons under Lou and Juliana Schmitt (946-8921) are Eric Abbatiello, Victoria Abbatiello, Mary Berestecky, Christine Beyer, Morgan Bondon, Danny Brenna, Timmy Costigan, Kari De Pol, Kristen De Pol, Brian Desmond, Carolyn Fee, Kathleen Fee, Jay Flynn, Linda Joyce, Joseph Joyce, Thomas Joyce, Colleen Keane, Steven Kopp, Maureen Mahoney, Kerry McCarthy, Maura McNamara, Jim Nugent, Ted Nugent, Patrick O'Malley, Christina Schaflin, John Schaflin, Amy Schmitt, Jim Schmitt, Donna Schweitzer, John Sheehan, Kate Sofronas, Tara Soldati, Vincent Sollecito, John Taltavall, Paul Taltavall, Mike Tolan, David Towne, Eileen Towne, Janet Usinski, Chung Vo, Hiep Van Vo, Anthony Wagar and Robert Walsh.

k. Banners are the work of Mary Ring (946-4750).

l. Flowers are arranged and cared for by Mary Rita Brennan, (431-3451), Marie Dooley, Elenmarie Dunn, Anita Gassert and Ann Hayes.

m. Church Maintenance under Juliana Schmitt (946-8921): Marie Abbatiello, Bea Abernathy, Mary Amory, Dolores Bacsik, Pat Biava, Dorothy Bills, Dorothy Conley, Eileen Connair, Joyce Connors, Pat Costigan, Julie Dalm, Jane Davis, Peggy De Pol, Sue Desmond, Ann DiFedele, Marie Dooley Agnes Duffy, Ellen Marie Dunn, Carolyn Flood, Betty Frank, Gisela Gray, Eileen Hand, Cathy Harrison, Roseanne Hazinski, Joan Henderson, Chris Hitchcock, Noreen Juliano, Eileen Kane, Kate Kristiansen, Mildred Lanzaron, Marge La Rue, Carolyn Le Munyon, Pat Madzin, Elaine Mc Mullin, Jane Meisner, Claire Merta, Margaret Miller, Louise Mistretta, Sophie Molnar, Evelyn Mosher, Dolores O'Malley, Helen Owendoff, Linda Rossano, Sandy Roy, Mary Schenone, Ann Scholtz, Carol Strnad, Angelica Syseskey, Suad Toutounchi, Mary Vanderbilt, Lorraine Walsh and Joan Ward.

n. Altar Linens are cared for by Dolores Bacsik (946-4250) and Ann Di Fedele (462-7718).

o. Altar Bread is baked by Dolores Bascik, Louise Basista, Marlene Berestecky, Theresita Blake, Mary Rita Brennan, Mary Byrne, Ann Di Fedele, Chris Durnan, Carolyn Flood, Mary Fournier, Alice Ganley, Nancy Joyce, Noreen Juliano, Ginny and John Marino, Linda McCarthy, Greta McFarland, Marilyn Morley, Evelyn Mosher, Barbara Schaflin, Julianna Schmitt and Madeline Tibbitt. Ginny Marino (946-8232) is chairperson of this group.

6. Record and Bulletin Binder: Alice Remmey (462-8761).

7. The Money Counters: Every Sunday several people count the collection after Masses. They give quiet, efficient service, a service as necessary as it is unsung. These people are Martha Ann Cicero, Walter Dowd, Joe Nichols and Fred Walling.

8. St. Mary's Youth Ministry is the coordinating committee for all of the high school age members of the parish. It seeks to provide opportunities for the youth to interact with each other in a variety of programs. It also provides opportunities for our youth to work closely with other parish organizations and committees. The Youth Ministry meets every Sunday evening at the parish hall under the direction of Geri Braden and the adult advisors.

9. The Family Life Committee coordinates the family life activities in the parish. Members are Sharon and Bill Burlew, Jane and Jack

9

Davis, Ellen and Ray Rugarber (462-2568) and Marie and Mike Steven.

10. The Religious Education Committee is under direction of Joanna Taltavall (780-2666). Eleanor Walsh is the secretary.

Coordinators: Mary Byrne, Jo Clement, Pat Costigna, Mary Germain, Fran Iadevaio, Betty Macron, Pat Marhan, Una McLeod, Carole Musci, Sandra Roy and Claire Stengel.

Cathechists: Carolyn Belena, Nancy Bell, Angela Berard, Beth Cicero, Janet Cichocki, Linda Damen, Colleen DeFelice, Peggy DePol, Susan Desmond, Richard Driber, Teddy Finan, Carolyn and Barney Flood, Bette Frank, Arlene Garito, Anita Gassert, Anneliese Germain, Mary Germain, Marilyn Grabowski, Lauretta Hangley, Paul Haupt, Mary Hazinski, Betty Kast, Beatrice Kelly, Sister Joan Koliss, Anne Marie LaRosa, Rita LaRosa, John Lonergan, Dorothy Mahoney, Meghan Mahoney, Arden Merwin, Rosemary McCann, Barbara McGovern, Tom Moroney, Helena Nugent, Cathy Prezzaman, Kathy Ross, Mary Schenone, Maura Schmidt, Fran Scudese, Millie Sollecito, Sharon Sturchio, Madeline Tibbitt, Jo Towne, Micki Vodarsik, Susan Wade, Jack Ward, Margie Whelan and Colette Gleim.

Substitutes: Judy Beitler, Joan Bowers, Sharon Burlew, Susan Davis, Mary Donnelly, Beth Finan, Cecilia Fitzpatrick, Gail Girard, Marilyn Howe, Doris and Tom Hudak, Roberta Kulesz, Millie Kunkel, Carol Link, Kay Neu, Lee Oberle, Meril Silipigni, Irene Willer, Maryellen Wigington.

11. Bible School: Jean Knipper (946-8633) is the coordinator. Catechists for the past year were: Ann Costanzo, Marian DeVesta, Pat Flood, Marjorie Gilbert, Christine Henderson, Joan Henderson, Jean Knipper, Laura Maggi, Diane Piotrowski, Eddie Piotrowski, Michael Piotrowski, Connie Reschke, Robin Reschke, Jeanine Rossano, John Taltavall, Paul Taltavall and Irene Weeler.

12. Evangelization: As the name itself implies the people involved in evangelization are seeking ways to bring the Gospel to those who find themselves on the margins of faith and the faith community. They are engaged in a geniune outreach for those who must be our parish concern. There are several areas of effort here under the direction of Barbara and Roger Kane (462-9391) and Eleanor Brady (542-7135).

a. The Calling Ministry Workshop: This is described in Part VI. It is a workshop consisting of two weekends (Friday evening and Saturday mornings) and six'Thursday evenings in October. Here trainings skills are given under expert leadership to approach, listen to and assist those who have left the faith.

b. Alienated Catholics: This is a reach out to those who have become disenchanted with the Church for one reason or another. We present two opportunities during the year for such people to come together to talk about their grievances and perhaps to find some help and answers. The first such meeting will be a special "An Invitation, Come Back Home" evening on October 7 from 8 to 10 p.m. This will be conducted by a special team from the Diocese as well as our own people. The program provides input from our own parish family as to whom we should reach out to — our neighbors and perhaps even members of our own family. Our second Alienated Catholics meeting will be held on March 24, and is open to all Catholics of the area who feel themselves alienated from the Church. A non-threatening, cordial meeting of great value is promised.

c. Parish Reach Out: As a result of the training received in the Caring Ministry workshop, the participants will go around to speak with and listen to the members of the parish who have become inactive and give them an opportunity to dialogue and, if they wish, to return to us. If they don't wish to return, they at least know of our concern and our prayers.

13. The Library: Coordinators are Ann Cokelet (264-5937) and Marge Whalen (431-3283). Members are Barbara Gieseking, Mary Latore, Helen Owendoff and Diane Piotrowski.

14. The Christmas Decorating Group: The Hyers Mill Neighborhood will decorate under the direction of Karen Greco and Judy Wilbert.

15. The Ministry of Hospitality: Here the parish gives welcome to all newcomers within the parish boundaries, Catholic or not, offering such people information about the churches and other organizations and just welcoming them, in the name of St. Mary's, to the area. Pat Biava (780-4785) is in charge.

16. Our Guest Book: Kept by Ann Scholtz (566-7927).

17. Goundkeepers under Jean Fitzgerald (431-0178) are Gail Giraud, Gisela Gray, Larry Herald, Bob Layton, Ginny and John Marino, the McCarthy Family, Diana and Ed Piotrowski, Herman Reyes, Nancy and Paul Runge, Mary Schenone, Ann Scholtz, Howard Somerville, Joan Uscinski, Lorraine Walsh and Walt, Irma and Mark Zimmerer.

Your neighbor as yourself

C. THE PARISH ORGANIZATIONS

1. The Martha and Mary Guild: This organization welcomes the company of ALL women of the parish. It provides the opportunity for those actively engaged in the spiritual, social and service life of the parish to become aware of and to support members' needs through shared ideas, prayer and sociability. Those unable to be active for one reason or another are cordially invited to attend the meetings on the second Wednesday of each month at 8 p.m. in the Parish Hall. Officers for this year are Kay Simone, President (462-8088), Jane Davis, Vice President, Helen Owendoff, Treasurer, Carol Strnad, Recording Secretary and Pat Madzin, Corresponding Secretary.

2. The Men's Parish Guild: This is a men's organization dedicated to the spiritual, physical and charitable needs of the parish. It sponsors the Labor Day Picnic and the Parish Cocktail Party and assists Father Bausch in any social or physical need that may arise. This group meets on the last Wednesday of each month in the Parish House. The officers are Bob Grabowski, President (431-2236), Joe George, Vice President, Don Voss, Treasurer and John Hambor, Secretary.

person to wear a name tag to church. We have gained lots of new people over the years and often our family members don't know each other. This way, especially at the sign of peace, we can get to know each other. don't look out of the corner of your eye, but straightforward, directly, at the tag. You'll get to know the names of all those people you see all the time at church and even say "hi" to, but don't know their names and dread it if you have to make introductions. so "Operation Name Tag" for September and October. It's a great way of affirmation.

C. THE CALLING MINISTRY:

This has nothing to do with Bell telephone, but everything to do with our first point: calling the inactive. fallen-away Catholic. But some training is needed for this and so we have that training in this six-part course given by Father Brietski and his associates. This schedule consists of two weekends (a Friday evening and Saturday morning) plus six sessions one evening a week from October 9 to November 21. Here professional training will be given in calling and listening. Listening skills which are valuable in all areas of life are applied here to our brothers and sisters in the Lord. If interested, call the parish office.

D. YOUTH MINISTER:

Parishes, like people, go through stages of infancy, childhood, adolescence, young adulthood and mature age. St. Mary's is through its infancy and childhood. We see this is the obvious change the parish commitment to them and to you in a very concrete way. Therefore, the parish, with the advice of the Parish, Council, has hired a full time Youth Minister, Geri Braden, to work with Father O'Brien and the Adult Advisors. She begins this September.

E. SPIRITUAL LIFE COMMITTEE:

This is a newly formed ministry dedicated to fostering our theme of affirmation. Those who are engaged in the many parish activities need to be reminded of their Source of inspiration, the main motivation of their dedication. They need to be rekindled in their spirits lest they burn out from lack of depth. That Source and Motivation is Jesus. The spiritual life ministry therefore provides both spiritual leaders and opportunities for the people to have evenings of recollection, days of retreat and prayer, either here or away, and general resources for the renewal of their spiritual lives. This is the greatest form of affirmation.

38

27 — Fr. Vernard's Prayer Group 10 (H & C); PRAY by Sr. Joan 10:30 (SC) WHERE'S FATHER SMITH by Fr. Bausch 8 (SC); Folk Choir 8 (C)

28 — Dance Exercise Class 9:45 (H); CHRISTIAN ORGINS: THE EARLY CENTURIES by Deacon A. Kevin Quinn 8 (SC); Social Gospel and Finance Committee groups Evening of Recollection (SC); Men's Guild 8:30 (HE)

29 — Scripture Sharing Group 10 (SC); Girl's Sex Ed 7:30 (HE); Calling Ministries Workshop 8 (SC); Choir 8 (C)

30 — Jack O'Lantern Celebration 7 (C & H); Calling Ministries Workshop Orientation Meeting 8 (SC)

NOVEMBER

1 — Pre-school 10:30 (HE); Youth Ministry 7 (H); All Saints Day

2 — Closed AA meeting 10 (HE); R.E. Classes grades 1-6 3:30 and grades 7, 8 and 9 7:30; all Souls Day

3 — Election Day 7 A.M. - 8 P.M.; Martha/Mary Board meeting 9:45 (HE); Children's Choir 4:15 (C); Learning Disability Group 7:30 (H); WHERE'S FATHER SMITH by Fr. Bausch 8 (SC); folk Choir 8 (C)

4 — Dance Exercise Class 9:45 (H); Fellow Pilgrims 12:30 (SC); PRAY by Sr. Joan 8 (SC); CHRISTIAN ORIGINS: THE EARLY CENTURIES by Deacon A. Kevin Quinn 8 (SC); Parents and Friends Association 8 (HE)

5 — Scripture Sharing Group 10 (SC); Moppet Choir 3:30 (C); Girl's Sex Ed 7:30 (HE); Parish Council 8 (SC); Choir 8 (C); Calling Ministries Workshop 8 (SC)

6 — First Friday: Mass 9 A.M.; Exposition; Healing Mass 8; Fifth grade girls' overnight retreat 7:45

7 — Monmouth County Deacons' Square Dance 8 (H)

8 — Pre-school 10:30 (HE); Teen Mass 5; Youth Ministry 7 (H); Single Experience 7:30 (SC); Baptismal Program 7:30 (SC)

9 — Samaritans 9:45 (H); Closed AA meeting 10 (HE); R.E. classes grades 1-6 3:30 and 7, 8 and 9 7:30; Neighborhood Visitation 8

10 — Seventh grade retreat at Collier School; PRAY by Sr. Joan 10:30 (SC); Children's choir 4:15 (C); WHERE'S FATHER SMITH by Fr. Bausch 8 (SC); Folk Choir 8 (C)

11 — Dance Exercise Class 9:45 (H); CHRISTIAN ORIGINS: THE EARLY CENTURIES by Deacon A. Kevin Quinn 8 (SC); Chinese Auction 8 (H); Veteran's Day

12 — Girl's Sex Ed 7:30 (HE); PM Table Talk 8 (SC); Calling Ministries Workshop 8 (SC); Choir 8 (C)

Parish Census

One of the first approaches to parish community is to find out the real needs of the people, their real opinions and thoughts, not the ones we think they have. To achieve this purpose several years ago, we came up with a census format. It had a basic tear-off page requesting statistical information; the other pages asked people's opinions on a variety of issues.

The format was quite defective in many ways and was hardly scientific. Still, it did prove valuable to us. We received many creative suggestions. From it, for example, we designed many programs for the parish and even rearranged our Mass schedule and the types of liturgical approaches to various Masses. This, after our Parish Booklet, is the most frequently requested publication. I hope the sample pages here give you an impression of what we were trying to do.

The whole census form may be obtained by writing to Census Form, St. Mary's Parish, Route 34, Colts Neck, N.J. 07722.

SECTION   I

This questionnaire is anonymous (no names please) so that you can respond as honestly as you can. Put a check mark next to the one (and only one) statement that best reflects how you feel. You'll notice that there are three sets of the same statements marked Person A, Person B and Person C. This is so that at least three people in your house can also express their opinion if they care to. Your census taker will pick up this questionnaire also -- unless you prefer to mail it in.

1. I find most meaning in attending Mass at:

Person A	Person B	Person C
___ St. Mary's	___ St. Mary's	___ St. Mary's
___ another local church	___ another local church	___ another local church
___ a local chapel or college campus	___ a local chapel or college campus	___ a local chapel or college campus
___ a church in another town	___ a church in another town	___ a church in another town

2. At Mass I most prefer:

Person A	Person B	Person C
___ no music	___ no music	___ no music
___ only organ music	___ only organ music	___ only organ music
___ the choir singing	___ the choir singing	___ the choir singing
___ folk music	___ folk music	___ folk music
___ congregational singing	___ congregational singing	___ congregational singing

1

3. I would most prefer to learn about my faith by:

Person A	Person B	Person C
___ reading more about it	___ reading more about it	___ reading more about it
___ through a sermon	___ through a sermon	___ through a sermon
___ attending parish lectures	___ attending parish lectures	___ attending parish lectures
___ discussion groups	___ discussion groups	___ discussion groups

4. The last time I talked with my parish priest in person or over the phone was:

Person A	Person B	Person C
___ in the past 2 days	___ in the past 2 days	___ in the past 2 days
___ in the past week	___ in the past week	___ in the past week
___ in the past month	___ in the past month	___ in the past month
___ in the past 6 months	___ in the past 6 months	___ in the past 6 months
___ in the past 5 or more years	___ in the past 5 or more years	___ in the past 5 or more years
___ never	___ never	___ never

5. The last time I went to Communion was:

Person A	Person B	Person C
___ in the past week	___ in the past week	___ in the past week
___ in the past month	___ in the past month	___ in the past month
___ in the past 6 months	___ in the past 6 months	___ in the past 6 months
___ in the past 12 months	___ in the past 12 months	___ in the past 12 months

2

11. The sermons given by Father Bausch at St. Mary's are generally:

Person A	Person B	Person C
___ very good	___ very good	___ very good
___ good	___ good	___ good
___ fair	___ fair	___ fair
___ poor	___ poor	___ poor
___ indifferent	___ indifferent	___ indifferent

12. The music at Mass (cantors, organists, congregational singing) is generally:

Person A	Person B	Person C
___ very good	___ very good	___ very good
___ good	___ good	___ good
___ fair	___ fair	___ fair
___ poor	___ poor	___ poor
___ indifferent	___ indifferent	___ indifferent

13. The lectors are generally:

Person A	Person B	Person C
___ very good	___ very good	___ very good
___ good	___ good	___ good
___ fair	___ fair	___ fair
___ poor	___ poor	___ poor
___ indifferent	___ indifferent	___ indifferent

14. The Parish CCD program is generally:

Person A	Person B	Person C
___ very good	___ very good	___ very good
___ good	___ good	___ good
___ fair	___ fair	___ fair
___ poor	___ poor	___ poor
___ indifferent	___ indifferent	___ indifferent

15. The banners, flowers, decorations for special feasts and occasions are generally:

Person A	Person B	Person C
___ very good	___ very good	___ very good
___ good	___ good	___ good
___ fair	___ fair	___ fair
___ poor	___ poor	___ poor
___ indifferent	___ indifferent	___ indifferent

16. The Parish Organizations (the Rosary Guild and Men's Guild) are generally:

Person A	Person B	Person C
___ very good	___ very good	___ very good
___ good	___ good	___ good
___ fair	___ fair	___ fair
___ poor	___ poor	___ poor
___ indifferent	___ indifferent	___ indifferent

17. I believe in:

    a) A Personal God   ___ yes   ___ no   ___ unsure

    b) Jesus as divine Son
        of God   ___ yes   ___ no   ___ unsure

    c) Heaven   ___ yes   ___ no   ___ unsure

    d) Sacraments as
        occasions of union
        with God   ___ yes   ___ no   ___ unsure

    e) God's assistance is
        available   ___ yes   ___ no   ___ unsure

    f) Jesus' resurrection   ___ yes   ___ no   ___ unsure

    g) Existence of hell   ___ yes   ___ no   ___ unsure

    h) Our redemption through
        Christ   ___ yes   ___ no   ___ unsure

    i) the Church as a
        community of believers   ___ yes   ___ no   ___ unsure

18. I have thoughts of agreement or disagreement with the following:

    a) responsibility to share with
        those who have less   ___ agree   ___ disagree

    b) responsibility to oppose
        injustice   ___ agree   ___ disagree

    c) moral convictions affect
        work   ___ agree   ___ disagree

    d) Church rules are no longer
        clear   ___ agree   ___ disagree

    e) Confused about Church's
        teachings   ___ agree   ___ disagree

    f) Church's rules are too
        inflexible   ___ agree   ___ disagree

And now, if you will, just a few fill-ins (where they apply). Other household members can copy these statements on another piece of paper and attach them to this if they wish.

19. Something I've always wanted to say to the pastor is this:

————————————————

————————————————

————————————————

————————————————

20. What do you think of the pastor?

————————————————

————————————————

————————————————

————————————————

21. What do you think of the Associate Pastor?   (Sister Claire)?

————————————————

————————————————

————————————————

————————————————

22. If you marked any of the preceeding pages as only fair, poor or indifferent, can you give suggestions for improvement? (Identify area)

————————————————

————————————————

————————————————

————————————————

23. I think the parish should: _____

_____

_____

_____

24. I think the biggest problem we the people have to face today is:

_____

_____

_____

_____

25. Something we never hear preached from the pulpit -- and we should
    -- is:

_____

_____

_____

_____

26. Given the rising cost of construction and the cost of energy do
    you think we should reconsider the erection of a Parish Center?

    ___ yes   ___ no

27. Any other comments?

_____

_____

_____

_____